Neurotic Distortion of the Creative Process

Neurotic Distortion of the Creative Process

Lawrence S. Kubie, M.D.

THE NOONDAY PRESS

A DIVISION OF

FARRAR, STRAUS AND GIROUX

First published in cloth by
the University of Kansas Press,
Porter Lecture Series No. 22

Published simultaneously in Canada
by Ambassador Books, Ltd., Toronto

Manufactured in the U.S.A.

Preface

This does not presume to be a book about what kinds of human beings are creative and what kinds become psychologically ill. Indeed I do not believe that anyone today knows quite enough to write such a book. What I have ventured is a more limited and modest study of those particular aspects of Man's symbolic processes which constitute the instrument both of his creativity and of his psychological illness. The hypothesis which motivated this study is that the interplay among these various aspects of the symbolic process determines in large measure the form and the fate of both the neurotic and the creative processes.

I have not hesitated to make this a technical study. Yet I hope that it will be understandable not only to the technician but also to the thoughtful reader who is not trained as a specialist in psychology, psychiatry, or psychoanalysis.

Contents

Chapter 1

The Psychodynamics of
Neurosis and Creativity

1. INTRODUCTION

This book will be divided arbitrarily into three parts.
It has three purposes, which will weave their ways through
the three chapters, knitting them, I hope, into a reason-
ably unified whole.

The Universality of Both Creativity and the Neurotic
Process

My first purpose will be to try to show that these
intertwined yet mortal enemies, the creative and the
neurotic processes, are universal; because both arise in
early childhood, not out of exceptional circumstances but
out of simple and ubiquitous human experiences. Subsequently these are reinforced by later stresses, among
which that which we euphemistically call education
plays an important role (cf. chapter III).

Creativity and Illness

My second purpose is to re-examine the old observation which links genius with insanity, creativity with illness (24, 57, 58, 59, 60). This observation, however
valid it may or may not be, has in itself no novel implications. Nor would I illuminate it if I were merely to add a
few additional biographical summaries of the lives of
men who were both creative and insane. Among the

1

earlier psychoanalytic studies the most illustrious examples are Freud's own hypotheses concerning Leonardo da Vinci (16), Gradiva (17), and Dostoevski (18). More recent examples are found in Sterba (73); and complete surveys of the relevant literature are available in Hitschmann (25), Hirsch (24), Ghiselin (19), Phillips (68), De Voto (10), Trilling (76), Kris (28), and Hoffman (26).

These chapters, however, will be concerned not with the concurrence of aberrations of mental illness among artists or other creative folk; nor with the creative productions of those who either were at the time, or had been, or subsequently became, deranged. Artists and scientists can fall ill in just as diverse ways as can the run-of-the-mill man who is not recognized as the possessor of any special creative gift. (Cf. Cane, F., 8; Naumburg, 63, 64, 65; Goitein, 20.) Whether this hypothetical common man is in fact as devoid of creative potential as is implied by this culturally snobbish convention is a point which will come into question as I develop my argument.

Implicit in the basic thesis that the creative and the neurotic processes are equally ubiquitous is a fact which should jolt our complacency, whether as scientist, artist, writer, painter, or musician: namely, that merely to be creative is not enough either to protect us from mental illness or to cure us. This should be no surprise if my contention is correct that potential creativity is as universal as the neurotic process. Nor should we be misled by the fact that under appropriately devised circumstances creative activities can be used as one ingredient in the therapeutic process. This does not mean that creative activity alone can ever cure.

Beethoven once wrote that in his opinion there is more wisdom to be found in music than in all of philosophy and science. This statement makes one think of Beethoven's lifelong inner struggles, torn with love and hate and suspicion and jealousy and rage, destructive to everyone whose life touched his, driving his nephew to an attempt at suicide, frequently as blocked in his musical creativity as in his life (Sterba, 73). Or one thinks of the suicides of certain successful writers, or of the permanent illnesses of certain creative scientists. And one recalls soberly that Van Gogh did not paint his way out of an asylum; and that neither dancing nor painting protected or cured Nijinsky. So one wonders whether Beethoven was not whistling out of the dark depths of his own illness, an illness which found no easement in the creative fire of his genius. Of certain modern artists and writers it is sometimes said that they protect themselves from psychoses by their painting or writing. Unfortunately, no critical studies exist which would make of such claims anything more than superficial and somewhat dubious guesses.

It is further sobering to consider the varied effects of that form of creative art which is the most universal of all: namely, the Dream. We dream ourselves into illness quite as often as out of it. Tausk described this many years ago (74). To go to sleep "well," and then to dream only to awaken ill was a frequent and tragic experience among combat troops during the war and among seamen of the Merchant Marine (4, 37, 38). Examples will be given below of dreams as art forms, products of the potentially creative psychological process which is inherent in all human life, and which is also an essential ingredient

3

in both the creative and the schizophrenic processes, yet bears no *constant* relation either to falling ill or to falling well. I emphasize this lack of any simple and constant correlation because I want to make it clear from the outset that this book will be concerned exclusively with the vulnerability of the creative *process* as such, and not with any hypothetical, special vulnerability of creative *people*, nor with any specious and oversimplified assumptions about the curative or preventive virtues of creative activity.

Instead we will consider the relationship between the creative and the psychopathological processes on a level which is both subtler and more general. My first effort will be to clarify the intrinsic reason for the association between the two processes in their most general sense, i.e., the mechanisms which are identical, their differences, and their interactions. If I can succeed in presenting an hypothesis which will clarify even a small part of this. and which can ultimately be subjected to experimental and clinical validation, my major purpose will be achieved.

Creativity without Illness

My third purpose takes as its point of departure another ancient cliché which unfortunately remains current today. This is the culturally noxious assumption, devoid as far as I can see of the least fragment of truth, that one must be sick to be creative. It is extraordinary to note how stubbornly this notion is defended. Many psychologically ailing artists, writers, musicians, and scientists, even including some individuals whose productivity may have been seriously impeded by their neuroses, refuse therapy out of a fear that in losing illness they will lose not only their much prized "individuality" but also their creative zeal and spark.[1] This is a curious position to defend; since instead of stressing their creativity, they imply that it is the artist's neurosis which is unique. Yet in reality the neurosis is the most banal and undistinguished component of human nature. This statement is true even for the symbolic language in which the neurosis expresses itself, whether in symptom, dream, or work of art or science.

Nevertheless insofar as men are reluctant to change, they unwittingly defend their neuroses. We want to be rid of our toothaches; but we do not want the process of getting well to make us "different" from whatever we are used to being. The creative man is not alone in defending himself (and therefore his neurosis) against change; but his recalcitrance receives special support from culturally accepted rationalizations. Buttressed by the legend that without illness the creative spark will die, scientists, artists, musicians, and writers tend as a group to be more resistant than other men. Of such refusals of therapy every psychiatrist could give many examples from his daily practice. Yet my own clinical experiences and also the weight of theory force me to take sharp issue with this

---

[1] At this point I want to interrupt my main argument to acknowledge without equivocation that psychotherapy, including psychoanalytic therapy, does not always succeed in removing the intra-psychic road-blocks to creativity. It succeeds under certain psychological circumstances, but fails under others. The major reason for this variability in therapeutic efficacy is the fact that the processes which can paralyze the creative activity of a writer, painter, composer, or scientist may be a manifestation of a wide variety of clinical conditions, masked or overt. Like a fever or a rash, such a symptomatic block can signify processes of illness so different that they could not be expected to yield with equal readiness to any one type of therapy. A detailed discussion of the conditions of therapeutic success and failure is not relevant to the issues with which we are concerned in these lectures.

position. Even allowing for the possibility that optimism may color my judgment, I nonetheless affirm my conviction that Man's actual creative productivity, as compared to his potential productivity, is pitifully reduced by the ubiquitous, masked, neurotic ingredients of what is euphemistically called "normal" human nature. Furthermore, the fragment of potential creativity which survives these neurotic inhibiting influences is first distorted in content and then is made rigid and stereotyped by these same veiled processes. What men succeed in creating is in spite of their struggles to overcome their neuroses, and not in any sense the fruit of these struggles. Of this many examples will be given below.

What is more, the residual creativity which survives this struggle is rendered culturally impotent, because the product is an ineffectual compromise between two processes. Thus the full price for the ubiquity of the neurotic process is paid not by the creative artist or scientist alone. Nor is it limited to those whose personal lives touch his. It is paid by all of society and by that very art, literature, music, or science to which the creative spirit attempts to contribute, and through which the artist struggles to live his life and to speak his piece in that life. The toll which neurosis exacts of Man's creative potential is paid by all human culture.

The implications of this position are realistic but not pessimistic. Indeed it implies to the contrary that when Man learns how to free his creative processes from the drag and bias of covert neurotic influences, he will have achieved the highest degree of spiritual freedom and the greatest cultural advance of which human nature is capable. He will stand at the frontiers of wholly new lands of Canaan.

The Dedication to Creativity

I should at this point make it clear that I am not going to explore the motivations of the artist, the writer, or the scientific investigator. I am not going to ask, "Why does one man paint or write or compose or play music [Boas, 5, 6, 7; Sachs, 71; Babbitt, 2], while another does scientific research in one field or another?" This is an important problem about which I have had something to say on another occasion (48); but it is not relevant to the issue to which I want to draw attention here: to wit, the dynamics of creativity and its vulnerability to distortion. Furthermore, it would be premature to explore the choice of the creative way of life until psychiatry has solved the more basic general problem of the "choice" of neurosis.

Consequently the creative life as such will not be our major concern here. Only one comment about it may be worth tucking away for future consideration. All activities which men think of as "Vocations" or "Callings" are those for which men feel themselves to be in some special fashion chosen, and to which they feel dedicated. This somewhat exalted frame of mind has never been adequately studied despite its subtle flavor of discreet megalomania, a megalomania which may be masked by outward humility, poverty, chastity, religious devotion, or dedication to a life of scientific research. There is an aura of myth and legend about all such vocations, and about those who follow the Road. The acceptance of the Vocation is always pictured as a response to one of two forces. One is "called" either by God or by the Devil; either for

7

a church and its works, or for Beelzebub and his. Those chosen by Beelzebub have included an interesting crew: devils and witches, the sorcerers and wizards who invoke or command them, priests and holy men, prophets and philosophers, alchemists and chemists. Over the centuries their modern descendants have evolved along several lines: religious leaders and philosophers, scholars and scientists, playwrights, actors and actresses, artists and musicians. We move from Bach to Bebop and back again; while all of the dangerous works of the theater, all of the graven images, all of the blasphemies of art, literature, and music have been profane when these works are not literally or figuratively for a church. Yet whether sacred or profane these activities remain Vocations; and those who labor in any of these fields are Dedicated Folk. One need talk only momentarily to the excited and hyper-snobbish devotees of modern jazz to sense their glazed dedication to a superior way of life. They, too, constitute a self-chosen Priesthood. The basic struggle between authoritarianism and freedom has been waged successively over the battlefields of religion, politics, and economics. The search to which the Chosen dedicate themselves has undergone a significant and parallel evolution. The scientist has moved from Absolutism to Relativity. In the arts, however, there has been a floundering and a splashing back and forth from one Absolute to another: from Absolutes of Form to the Absolutes of an apparent Formlessness, which in reality can have unconscious meanings as precise and literal as anything in representational art, whether or not the creating artist senses their true nature. This increasing emphasis in science on the relativity of truth, and in art, music, and literature on Form which is

8

unstructured, leads inescapably to one destiny, namely, to the expression of that which is buried deepest in human nature. Yet this is something which the creative man has only rarely had either the technical knowledge or the introspective insight to recognize. The writer and artist may believe that he is expressing the World's Neurosis: but in reality the very essence of his 1957-Model Vocation is his unwitting dedication to the expression of his own Neurosis for all the world to see. Equally without realizing it, the psychologist who studies only lower animals or men other than himself may also be using his form of science as an evasive substitute for looking squarely at himself. Yet to express our own illness is not merely a privilege: it is a supreme duty, a calling, and a destiny if the human spirit is to make any significant progress. We must share with others our innermost conflicts in our art, music, literature, and science for others to feel with us. Otherwise the creative spirit will perpetuate its neuroses in its Science, or in Psychoanalysis, or in one of the many "modern" versions of art for art's sake, or in one or another form of religion; since the neurotic process can misuse all of these. The future confronts us with the supremely important task of learning how to communicate through the fog of Mankind's fears the facts about Man's age-old struggle with the universal concealed neurotic process.

When I consider how long and arduous is the task of making the truth an effective living reality even to just one human patient, who has been driven by his own suffering to seek the truth about himself and his life, then I must confess that the difficulties sometimes seem insurmountable which confront any effort to use art and litera-

9

ture and music as a vehicle for making truth meaningful to many. In such moments of discouragement even the best of poetry and fiction seems a watering down and disguising of truth so as to make it palatable, as though truth were too strong a drink for human palates. If this is true, then it may be fair to say that literature and art weaken the truth to enable many people to accept some fragments of it; whereas psychoanalysis attempts to strengthen one individual to the point at which he will be able to face and to accept the whole truth. Yet no form of art or education has found out how to increase the receptive strength of Man in general. Perhaps this is the ultimate challenge which is faced today by education and by all cultural processes.

These reflections apart, my purpose is not to make invidious distinctions among the unwritten dedications to which the man who is "called" inscribes his life; but merely to insist that among those who strive to be creative the sense of dedication is always present, no matter how it is masked by a matter-of-fact and workaday attitude, by generosity or selfishness, by arrogance or humility. These are always present, intermingled in varying proportions.

Devotees to different gods seem fated always to clash over whose gods are the most powerful. They join forces only when some outsider dares to doubt the magical power of all of them. Since I am just such an outsider to the arts, there is no escaping the fact that much of what I shall say will be resented. Yet no mature consideration of the problem can turn its back on certain facts: (1) that a clarification of the role of neurosis in human life is at once the most pressing yet the least acknowledged challenge which confronts human culture; (2) that the creative spirit today is struggling blindly and confusedly to accept this challenge, and (3) that consequently all of art and literature today deal with the neurotic in human nature. This state of affairs does not, however, warrant the usual, if quite illogical, assumption that illness is necessary to the creative act. The fact remains that the processes of illness block and corrupt the creative act. Moreover, just as illness produces neurotic symptoms which becloud the very conflicts which they aim to express, so the creative product of science and the arts can mask and disguise the very processes of illness to the clarification and expression of which modern art, literature, music, and science are currently if unwittingly dedicated. This indeed is the paradoxical dilemma of the precise moment of culture through which we are passing (51).*

The Sources of My Approach

The sources of most of the data which I shall present are psychoanalytic, in that they are solidly based on the essentials of psychoanalytic fact, theory, and technique. Fortunately, however, this book will not deal with any of the controversial and overelaborated current modes of psychoanalytic thought and terminology. This is not an appropriate occasion for a technical discussion of the pros and cons of various psychoanalytic theories of creativity. Moreover, having studied these theories with some care for many years, I find myself happier with certain of the earlier psychoanalytic formulations, because they remain closer to the realities of clinical observation and are more accessible to experimental correction and confirmation. Consequently for the purposes of my discussion it will not be necessary to deal with those developments of psychoanalytic theory and terminology which Freud called its "economic" aspects (by which he meant quantitative variables). Nor will we deal with its structural aspects (by which he meant the allocation of different functions to different facets of the personality). This will also spare us the necessity of burdening the reader with a clutter of references to the literature, solely for the purpose of demonstrating historical erudition. My references will be sparse and largely non-psychoanalytic, except for the few key and original contributions.

We must, however, describe the basic facts about the ways in which human psychological processes operate. These psychoanalytically derived data constitute the conceptual basis for all that follows. This will include a discussion of what we mean by normality, by creativity, and by the neurotic process. The illustrative diagrams are not to be taken literally. They do not represent measurable quantities of force. They are visual schemata, pictograms without which the meaning of certain basic abstract concepts would remain obscure.

2. The Neurotogenic Universals

Fortunately, it is not necessary to undertake a detailed exposition of the neurotic process in its entirety (44, 46). For my thesis it is essential only to show why there is any justification for stating flatly that its distorting influence both on human lives and on human creativity is universal. Actually this is because there is a neurotic potential that is inherent in the structure of the human psyche (50) and because out of this universal potential the neurotic process is set in motion and shaped by experiences that are universal in infancy and early child-hood, and not by exceptional or even specially stressful circumstances, however dramatically these may influence its later evolution. Were all of this not true, the neurotic process could not be universal.

I have in mind many events which occur daily in every life, and which are familiar to us in every culture. They shape our personalities, our potentials for psychological health or illness, and our potential creativity. Yet just because of their familiarity, their importance for human development has been largely overlooked. A further implication is that if we are ever to learn how to prevent or at least to lessen the insidious destructive influence of the neurotic process, we shall have to re-examine the minutiae of the early steps of personality development, not when these are complicated by adverse environmental circumstances but in fortunate and benign situations.

Among the early external experiences which are universal and inescapable are the basic experiences of *dif-ferences*: the sharp changes in motion, sound, temperature, and light to which the human infant is incessantly exposed during his days as a Lilliputian in a world of seemingly eternal and Brobdignagian giants. Later come the toddler's encounters with further differences in size, bulk, weight, consistency; and also with the differences between those things which are and are not movable, which are hard and soft, rough and smooth, sharp and blunt, hot and cold.

Interwoven with the developmental experiences of an inner and outer world and adding to their complexity are other daily experiences which slowly bridge the gap between these two worlds. To take alien things from the outer world into that strange and mysterious bodily machine which ultimately signifies "Me" becomes at some point an overwhelming experience for every child. The concomitant daily experiences of bringing products forth from that Body and of casting them off into the outer world of limitless space become equally strange and mysterious.

These universals are among the child's disturbing, primary encounters with reality, about which our elementary symbolic potential develops. To them are added other disturbing experiences of body differences with respect to size, shape, smell, color, and hairiness, and especially, of course, the differences in all secondary sexual characteristics.

To none of these differences have men ever become fully reconciled, either in the course of individual lives, or through the history of human culture. This fact is one of the great unsolved conundrums of human development. Many claims are made, backed by fragmentary bits of evidence, about the inheritance of psychological quirks or even of specific ailments. Yet such homely experiences as these are repeated uncountable times in ontogeny and in philogeny, without becoming part of our innate endowment. How does it happen that such basic components of human life have not left clear, uncomplicated, familiar, conflict-free and effort-free traces in every human child? Instead, as generation succeeds generation, the lessons of these experiences are rejected with pain and are relearned with distortions. Indeed, with every new human life they are rejected and denied anew. In each they evoke irreconcilable surges of buried thoughts and feelings, which are expressed in disguised forms through symptoms, nightmares, and dreams, or in myths, legends, religious rituals, and taboos, or through art, song, and story, or in systems of pseudo-aesthetics, or in fashions and cosmetics and in culturally endorsed defenses such as scientific research, or other compensatory activities too numerous to list. Yet in spite of all of this they remain perpetually unfamiliar, as perplexing and frightening to each new human generation as though no previous child had encountered them. Throughout our entire lives we spend a substantial part of our energies struggling to master these universal experiences by devious and unsatisfactory efforts to deny them. Furthermore, this unconscious effort to deny or to reconcile differences makes up no small part of the content of neurotic symptoms, of art and of science.

To these daily increments, which slowly build the child's conceptualizations of an inner and outer world, are added repeated experiences of *meetings with* and of *partings from* both the familiar and the strange (Spitz, 72).

Paralleling all of these confused efforts to deal with the elementary and universal ingredients of human life is another fundamental and recurring tidal process, the understanding of which is of equal importance to our understanding of the relation of creativity to illness. This is the dramatic daily transition into and out of sleep. These daily transits have special and often critical effects, which are noxious quite as often as they are restorative (37, 40, 41). They are important in the genesis both of creativity and of illness; because during these transitions through varied states of consciousness all of these universal experiences are re-experienced in dreamlike symbolic representations, altered, fragmented, reworked, distorted, lost, recaptured, resynthesized, and in some measure digested. We find their traces in dreams, in reveries, and in pseudo-hallucinatory and hypnagogic states, as well as in the products of science and of art. Furthermore, this happens every day and every night in every human life. The universality of the symbolic content of dreams rests upon the universality of these inescapable ingredients of human development.

I have listed only a few of the early experiences which are common to the lot of all men, and which enter into the development of both the creative and the neurotic processes, by providing much of the primitive content of both. These are the banal universals which are the overlooked building blocks of Man's creativity and of his neurotic illnesses. Rare and exceptional stresses add important complications to the effects of inescapable experiences; but these remain the roots. Perhaps it is precisely because they are universal that we have paid so little attention to them, have so underestimated both their creative and their destructive potential, and have left unsolved even at this late date in the history of human culture the problem of how to guide human infancy and childhood through Hänsel and Gretel's forest of Frightening Familiars.

These primitive and universal experiences demand appropriate reactive adjustments in the course of which we generate concepts and affects on various levels. And it is precisely here that human neurosis and human creativity have their origins: their evolution depending upon the levels on which these basic experiences are worked through and digested, and on the dissociations which develop in the process.

Thinking, feeling, and activity in infancy and earliest childhood, as in the lower animals, are so intertwined as to be inseparable; and their early development and organization proceed hand in hand. As a consequence during this very brief early stage in his development man can be neither creative nor neurotic. Dissociation among feelings, conceptualizations, and action is essential for psychological development. If they always went together, little psychological maturation of any kind could occur; but dissociations soon supervene, with results that will be discussed in the next section. All that need be said here is that both the creativity potential and the neurotic potential arise out of our strictly human ability to make patchy dissociations among them.

The development of activity also has a special relevance here. Activity starts in infancy with random, tentative, or explosive and largely undirected acts. At first these occur in response more to internal promptings than to external stimuli. The organization of these fragmentary movements into goal-directed and purpose-serving patterns depends upon three things, each of which leaves a lasting imprint on the structure of our psychological processes, an imprint which in turn is related directly both to creativity and to neurosis.

(1) The infant learns his basic patterns of behavior and expression at first through repetition (a matter to which we will return in Chapter III) and later through automatic (preconscious) imitation.

(2) The infant intermingles his *perceptual* responses to the outside world with his percepts of his inner world

(30, 44). Only slowly does he become able to separate these two worlds; and only later still can he begin to divide them into recognizably familiar and constant configurations of those percepts which mean on the one hand himself, his body, its parts, its processes, and on the other hand discrete external objects such as faces, sounds, people, and things. The gradual differentiation between the worlds of inner and of outer experience leads to the recognition of individual units of experience within each.

(3) As patterns of activity develop in the infant, a critical role is played by automatic (later we will call this "Preconscious") imitations of the movements, facial expressions, and sound of objects in the outer world, both human and infra-human, both animate and inanimate. In this way are acquired the unwitting imitations of expressions, postures, and meaningful gestures which so often turn small children into endearing, amusing, and mocking pocket-editions of their elders.

Thus in a variety of ways the infant slowly learns to use whole patterns of behavior. At first this is an automatic process. Later these patterns are organized into integrated and purposeful constellations, which return to partially automatic controls. Similarly, thought and feeling develop through comparable stages: i.e., first groping, random, automatic ("preconscious") imitative fragments, then integrated configurations under some degree of voluntary and purposeful control, and finally a partial return to more automatic usage.

Both creativity and neurosis are linked to this progression from automatic fragments of behavior to purposeful and synthesized acts, and then back again to a more automatic use of these syntheses; because it is during these transitions that we dissociate the various ingredients of affects, thoughts, behavior, and percepts from one another. Such dissociations become manifest in obligatory repetitions of various fragments of behavior which are uniquely characteristic of all manifestations of the neurotic process: affects segregated from appropriate thought or action, action segregated from content or affect, conceptual content segregated from affect and its appropriate expression in action. A comparable dissociation among these basic ingredients of behavior occurs in the creative process as well. Consequently that which is common to both is also something which is uniquely human, i.e., a *disturbance in the relation of the symbolic process to whatever it represents.* As a result of this disturbance in the relation of the symbol to its substratum, all human psychological processes ("mentation") fall into one of three categories. These are called, not too satisfactorily, "conscious," "preconscious," and "unconscious." Because these terms are historically well entrenched, we will continue to use them, for the time being at least: and will describe them quite fully in section 4 of this chapter. Subsequently our attention will turn to the interplay between *Preconscious* and *Unconscious* processes: since the vulnerability of creativity to neurosis depends particularly upon the relation between these two aspects of mentation, explained later.

3. THE NEUROTIC PROCESS

I am not going to contrast normal men with neurotic men, or normal cultures with neurotic cultures. I want to characterize merely the essential differences between a *single normal* and a *single psychopathological* act or moment of human life. It is important to keep this sharply circumscribed purpose in mind; because until we can agree on a characterization of what constitutes the essential psychopathology of a single psychological event, we will hardly be able to agree upon what constitutes psychopathology in a total personality, or in any group of individuals which we call a society or a culture, or in the relation of psychopathology to creativity.

There is not a single thing which a human being can do or feel, or think, whether it is eating or sleeping or drinking or fighting or killing or hating or loving or grieving or exulting or working or playing or painting or inventing, which cannot be either sick or well. Furthermore, to which category any act belongs will depend not upon conformity to any cultural norm; not on the frequency of the act in any society (since statistical frequency of colds or dental caries has nothing to do with whether they are sick or well); not on whether an act, feeling, or thought seems superficially to be sensible or foolish, useful or valueless, constructive or destructive. Nor does the distinction depend upon any such legal artifice as whether the individual knows the difference between right or wrong: since the psychotic and the criminal may have as clear judgments on moral issues as any clergyman. The measure of health is flexibility, the freedom to learn through experience, the freedom to change with changing internal and external circumstances, to be influenced by reasonable argument, admonitions, exhortation, and the appeal to emotions; the freedom to respond appropriately to the stimulus of reward and punishment, and especially the freedom to cease when sated. The essence of normality is flexibility in all of these vital ways. The essence of illness is the freezing of behavior into unalterable and insatiable patterns. It is this which characterizes every manifestation of psychopathology, whether in impulse, purpose, act, thought, or feeling. As I have said elsewhere (50), "Whether or not a behavioral event is free to change depends *not* upon the quality of the act itself, nor upon its individual or social consequences, but upon the nature of the constellation of processes that have produced it. Any moment of behavior is neurotic *if the processes that set it in motion predetermine its automatic repetition*, and this irrespective of the situation or the social or personal values or consequences of the act." Whenever psychological processes predetermine the tendency automatically to repeat, they are psychopathological. This applies to the businessman, artisan, or laborer, to the scientist or artist, and to everything each of them does. In the next section we will discuss what configuration of processes can predetermine the automatic repetition of behavior; since these are the storm centers of dreams and of illness to which the creative process is vulnerable.

There is conclusive evidence that in the human being psychological processes always function in three concurrent systems which resemble bands on a nearly continuous spectrum. Frequently these are spoken of as three "levels"; but all words which are used to describe them are figures of speech, and can lead to fallacious reasoning unless they are used carefully as descriptive allegorical devices. About them it is clear: (1) that conscious, preconscious, and unconscious psychological processes always operate concurrently and in varying patterns; (2) that we approximate most closely to normality when among them the preponderant influence is exercised by what one may call an alliance of conscious and preconscious processes; and (3) that we operate in the shadow of illness whenever unconscious processes are dominant. These three statements rest firmly on a large array of experimental and clinical data.

It is true that clinical observations first alerted Freud to the importance of this tripartite arrangement; but to imagine that the hypothesis derives solely from imprecise clinical observations would be wholly untrue. The types of data which validate these statements consist of (1) the experimental induction of neurotic states under hypnosis (34); (2) experimental work with differentiated preconscious perceptions during sleep (39); (3) experiments on the preconscious reactions to fleeting images on the tachistoscope of Charles Fisher (14), Lindley (56), Marsh and Worden (61); (4) experiments under hypnosis on the symbolic representation of repressed amnesic material (33); (5) the self-translating data of childhood during those phases in which language symbols are being formed (44); (6) data from schizophrenics with simultaneous

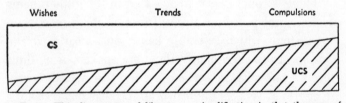

Wishes   Trends   Compulsions

CS

UCS

FIG. 1. This diagram is a deliberate oversimplification in that the area of preconscious processes (PCS) is omitted, so as to clarify the interplay between conscious (CS) and unconscious (UCS) functions.

Every human thought or feeling or act or pattern of living falls somewhere along such a continuous spectrum as this. The technical and quantitative problem is to determine where. It will be noted that the diagram indicates that there are no acts in which UCS processes play no role, and no acts which are devoid of CS determinants. If this is true, then in all probability the ends of the scale are theoretical abstractions.

multiple levels of meaning in symptoms, speech, action, and posture, etc. (47, 55).

4. THE THREE SYSTEMS OF SYMBOLIC FUNCTION*

The Conscious System of Symbolic Function

In the waking state Conscious symbolic processes are predominantly although not exclusively verbal. They are like the various items in a literal photograph, in a representational painting, in a simple factual story, in a programmistic dance, or in a toy. They make use of sounds, facial expressions, gestures, postures, movements, drawings, and plastic shapes as well as words; but the primary purpose is communication, to share experiences, memories, plans, and ideas. To a limited degree their purpose is also to share the attendant emotions. In poetry, fiction, and exhortation this effort to share conscious emotion through the conscious symbolism of speech plays a larger role; although even here this is limited by the fact that words tend automatically to mask and screen the emotional component of memory (47).

Conscious symbols are also used to characterize similarities among disparate experiences. Indeed it is only by generalizing from comparable experiences that we can form abstract concepts. Thus even the name of some banal object such as a chair is a symbolic representative of an abstraction formed from experiencing many chairs: high chairs and slipper chairs, rocking chairs and desk chairs, chairs for chairmen and electric chairs, musical

---

*The instrument for both rumination and communication in the Conscious and Unconscious Systems is the symbolic word, expression, sound or gesture. The instrument of rumination (i.e., intra-machine processing) in the Preconscious System is the "coded signal" of the communication engineer. The significance of these differences will be developed elsewhere (55).

chairs and chairs as the weapon of an angry man or of a lion-tamer. The symbol for a chair can set echoes reverberating down many mental corridors, all of which are tagged by the coded symbol "chair." Furthermore, the symbol can be a model of a chair, a toy, a drawing, the word, or the thing itself. Obviously we cannot and do not "think of" all of these connotations every time we use the word "chair." Yet they are not "unconscious" (v.i.). They are lurking in the wings where they are accessible on need. These other meanings are in the fringes of consciousness of which William James wrote and which we now call preconscious (v.i.). From the context and goal of our thought flows a process of automatic (preconscious) selectivity which excludes those meanings which are irrelevant to our central focus: but although we may shut the doors of thought against them, the affects which these fringe meanings evoke remain active. Consequently even as we sit unthinkingly on a banal kitchen chair, there will be some affective stirring from these collateral meanings of the concept "chair," like the sound of distant music.

Obviously all such verbal symbols are time-savers. We do not have to find a chair and point to it or sit in it, or to draw one in order to communicate the fact that we are thinking about a chair. In this way words perform an economizing function. Nevertheless when compared to the fantastic speed of the wordless processing of the same concept in preconscious thought, the conscious verbal symbol as used to communicate ideas is relatively slow and pedestrian. In fact the conscious level of symbolic function is a relatively slow vehicle of mentation, precisely because its primary purpose is not for thinking but for that slow-motion sampling of preconscious thought processes which we call communication ("speech"). We can *think* of many things at a time "preconsciously" (indeed at that level it is not possible to think of only one thing at a time): but we can *communicate* only one meaning at a time, if we hope to communicate clearly. Consequently even though the symbolic representation of concepts is an economizer, communication by means of conscious symbols must be far slower than are those wordless preconscious processes, a sample of whose net results we communicate in speech.

Furthermore, in the steps by which the child acquires speech, each verbal unit becomes increasingly differentiated as it matures. During the early steps in this process, the symbols which represent discrete objects have multiple meanings (30, 44). With added years more words are learned until nearly every informational unit (or bit) has its own coded verbal signal. On conscious levels these signals are restricted to the representation of only a few individual items. Consequently in adult speech all that is left of early, multiple meanings of words are such residues as occur in puns, slang, and allegory. Often these persist largely because they are hybrid heirs of diverse ancestry. An example would be the word "ball" for a round object, "ball" for a dance, and "ball" in current teen-age slang for having a "high old time," itself a bit of antique slang to which nostalgia has given an almost poetic flavor. This process by which we progress from immature levels of conceptual and symbolic function to maturity is represented schematically in Figure 2.

During the incessant and continuous fluctuations in the state of consciousness which occur during the waking

Maturation of the Symbolic Process
Immaturity ⟶ Maturity

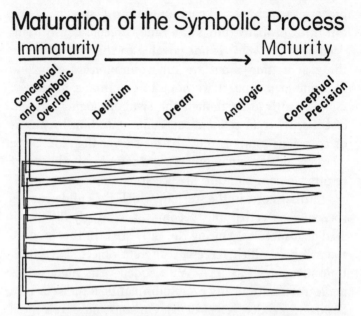

FIG. 2. The left margin of the diagram represents the period in early childhood when concepts are forming and are first receiving symbolic representation. The broad and overlapping bases at the left of the triangles are intended to represent the imprecision both of the early conceptual units and of their symbols. One result of this is the familiar fact that when a child first learns to use sounds as larval words, they cover many and varied conceptual units of experience. Subsequently as the processes of concept-formation and of their symbolic representation mature, we pass through successive phases. There is a gradual acquisition of multiple alternative symbols to represent single conceptual units; until as we reach greater precision (represented in the right-hand margin of the diagram) the link between concept and symbol approaches but never reaches an exclusive one-to-one relationship.

These phases in the process of maturation are roughly comparable to the types of thinking to which we return in delirium and in dreams and that which is used most freely in the analogical thinking of all creative processes. The type of thinking which characterizes one or another of these phases can be recognized both in illness and in health, in neurosis and in creative states, in conscious waking states, in sleep, in the dream, and in those various organic disorganizations of thought and speech in which there is partial regression to earlier stages in the development of language. It is this continuity in the symbolic process which makes it essential to have one term to cover all of its manifestations.

state, during sleep, and in all transitions between the two, there is a concomitant play of dissociative and reintegrative processes, with a continuous movement to and fro between immature and mature levels of symbolic function. Because of its relevance to creativity I would re-emphasize for future reference the fact that these shifts occur during the processes of falling asleep and of waking, in hypnagogic and fully hypnoidal processes and states (39), in abstracted states and states of maximally focused attention, under the influence of alcohol and of other drugs which affect cortical and/or emotional processes, and in toxic-delirious processes (40).

The Unconscious Levels of Symbolic Functions

At the other end of our spectrum of symbolic functions are what are loosely called "unconscious" processes. This is a misleading bit of technical jargon; because it is not the symbol that we employ which is unconscious, but only that which it represents. Here the word or image (i.e., the "coded signal") is a front for an unknown. At this symbolic level words play a less dominant role, since in a condensed manner they actually disguise the multivalent, fragmentary, sensory after-images of those past experiences which they purport to represent. In sleep these after-images are predominantly the visual hieroglyphics of the dream, each of which represents multiple and complex mental events and processes while at the same time striving to disguise them. Whether asleep or awake, they may be accompanied by bodily sensations (both enteroceptive and proprioceptive) or by detached emotional experiences, or by isolated words or actions. Therefore all such hieroglyphics represent complex pat-

27

terns of several concurrent unconscious meanings, super-imposed one upon another.[2]

Yet even complex constellations of conflict-laden and repressed ideas, feelings, memories, and purposes may be expressed simultaneously by some one mental scratch-mark, or by a brief sequence of images. That is why in a dream, a horse or a lamb or a fire or an automobile or an individual or a street or a pain will represent not merely one but many and frequently conflicting condensations of experiences, centering around many people and widely separated times and places. This is also how, in the waking state, one neurotic symptom can have similarly complex and multiple patterns of disguised meanings. In turn, this is why we are justified in saying that the state of illness is close to being a waking process of dreaming; and that the symptoms of psychological illness are analogous to the manifest content of a dream; and also that the production of a dream, or of symptoms of illness, or of the form and content of any art work all have many essential elements in common.

At this point I will try to clarify my meaning further by another figure (Fig. 3). From this, for purposes of simplification, I still omit any representation of the role of preconscious functions. I have drawn the diagram as

---

[2] That we can perceive, record, and reproduce without becoming conscious at any point has been proved repeatedly. All of this was long spoken of as unconscious. It now seems probable that most of this, if not all, is more accurately characterized as preconscious; in which case the labored discussion about whether there is anything in "the unconscious" which has not previously been conscious can be relegated to the past.

There has also been much discussion of the possibility that unconscious processes may be enriched by direct contributions from racial experiences which may never have been conscious. On this the evidence is far from conclusive; and the dynamically active unconscious which is our concern here is that which has at one time been conscious or preconscious but has been actively repressed so as to obscure an area of painful conflict.

though human mentation consisted solely of conscious and unconscious processes in a graded relationship like a continuous spectrum. The purpose of this oversimplification is to show how and why the behavior which results from a preponderance of conscious processes is, as I have already explained, flexible, adaptable, satiable, capable of learning from experience, admonition, exhortation, and instruction; whereas at the other end of this same spectrum, where the identical act may be produced by a constellation of processes among which unconscious processes predominate, the resultant behavior will be rigid, stereotyped, and insatiable, unmodifiable by the experience of success or failure, by rewards and punishments, by admonition or exhortation. Evidently at one end we have the essence of normal behavior; and at the other, the essence of sick behavior.

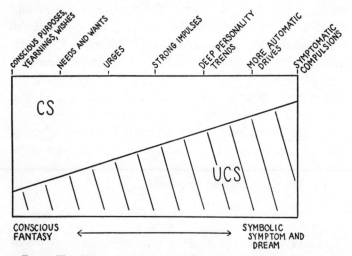

FIG. 3. This diagram is also an oversimplification in that it omits preconscious processes; but it extends the implication of the balance between CS and UCS processes from the area of symptom formation to more general drives and personality traits.

29

In order to clarify how and where creative functions operate between these two poles, we must interpose another type of mental process between the Conscious and Unconscious process. It is so important to be clear about this that I will paraphrase what I have said elsewhere about the nature and function of these "levels," or "systems" or "bands" in the more or less continuous spectrum which constitutes our symbolic functions.

There is the realistic form of symbolic thinking in which we are clearly aware of the relationship of the symbols of language to that which we intend to represent. Here the function of the symbol is to communicate the hard core, the bare bones of thought and purpose. This is conscious symbolic function.

At the other end of our spectrum is the symbolic process in which the relationship between the symbol and what it represents has been either distorted or completely ruptured by an active process of dissociation in time and place between affect and its occasion, which results in that dissociation between symbol and its root, which leads to what is called "repression." As a consequence, the symbol here is a disguised and disguising representative of unconscious levels of psychological processes. In this area the function of the symbolic process is not to communicate but to hide, not deliberately but automatically, and not only from others but even more urgently from ourselves. This is the unconscious symbolic process as it occurs in dreaming and in psychological illness.

Preconscious Process

There is however another type of mentation whose relationship to its roots is figurative and allegorical. The function of this intermediate form of mentation is

30

to express at least by implication the nuances of thought and feeling, those collateral and emotional references which cluster around the central core of meaning. Here every coded signal has many overlapping meanings; and every item of data from the world of experience has many coded representatives. This is the form of coded language which is essential for all creative thinking, whether in art or science. Therefore we will have much more to say about it below. In technical jargon, this second type of symbolic process is called *preconscious*.

At every moment of life, all three are active concurrently. As a consequence, whether we are sick or well everything we ever do or say or think or feel is a composite resultant of them all. This is true not only in dreams and symptoms of illness, and not only during our preoccupations with the banal daily chores of life, but in moments of our greatest creative achievement. Consequently when a scientist is studying atomic energy or a biological process or the chemical properties of some isotope, when a sociologist studies the structure of government and society, when a historian studies the development of great events, or an economist the play of economic forces, when a classicist studies an ancient tongue, or a musicologist the intricacies of musical composition, or when a theologian studies theology, each deals with his subject on all three of these levels at once. On the *conscious* level he deals with them as communicable ideas and approximate realities. On the *preconscious* level he deals with swift condensations of their multiple allegorical and emotional import, both direct and indirect. On the *unconscious* level, without realizing it, he uses his special competence and knowledge to express the conflict-laden

31

and confused levels of his own spirit, using the language of his specialty as a vehicle for the outward projection of his own internal struggles. Since this happens without his knowledge, it is a process which even in his own field can take over his creative thinking, distorting and perverting it to serve his unconscious needs and purposes, precisely as happens in a dream or in the symptom formations of neurotic and psychotic illness. I will give illustrations of these relationships and distortions below.

5. More about the Preconscious System

The Composition of the Preconscious

Because it is central to my thesis I must explain the several components which comprise preconscious processes in human psychology.[3]

First, perhaps, are those which become preconscious through the learning process and only *after* having been in some measure at least conscious.

These are an inevitable outcome of the learning process. They drop out of the central focus of conscious awareness not as the result of any processes of dynamic repression but through the repetition which is essential to the early steps by which we learn anything. Even those simple activities which are vital to life itself, such as breathing, sucking, excreting, moving, and crying, start as random and often explosive acts (55). The ability to execute them purposefully and economically is acquired (i.e., "learned") through repetition, in the

---

[3] This is paraphrased and elaborated from "The Concept of Normality and Neurosis," Chapter I, pp. 3-14, of *Psychoanalysis and Social Work*, edited by Marcel Heiman, M.D., International Universities Press, New York, 1953 (46), and from a lecture on Preconscious Processes before the American Academy of Neurology in Boston on April 23, 1957 (in press, 55).

course of which they become economically organized into goal-directed synergistic patterns which include somato-sensory, somatomuscular, and autonomic components. At first all of these activities are triggered by biochemical warning and prodding devices, which operate at this stage in the absence of any symbolic representation. In each instance, however, the *goals* of even the simplest acts soon acquire symbolic representation; and from that moment on in the human being symbolic processes begin to play continuously on the simple physiological mechanisms (52).

Once any such act is fully learned, it can be initiated quite independently of inner physical prodding merely by contemplating the goal. As this happens the entire constellation is triggered as a unit by the symbol which represents the goal; and we thereupon become unaware of the innumerable intermediate steps which make up the act. Their elimination from the field of conscious-ness is the great economy which is achieved in the process of learning by repetition. Indeed, this is probably the major if not the only *normal* function of repetition in the learning process. It is in this way that we become able to walk without pondering each step, to talk without having each time to work out anew the movements by which we enunciate each word. It is in this way that the violinist, the juggler, and the athlete learn complex chains of synergic movements. It is in this way that our thinking processes acquire the ability to leap over many interven ing steps as we perform complex arithmetical processes. Moreover, this is the root of intuitive thinking, whether in science or the arts.

It is worth re-emphasizing the fact that in each in-stance the intermediate steps drop into the background and disappear from the center of consciousness into what we call the Preconscious System. Here, in sharp contrast to the Unconscious System, Preconscious processes remain accessible on need and with varying degrees of effort to conscious self-examination. What William James called the "fringe of consciousness" is what Freud called *preconscious*, as contrasted with a dynamic *unconscious*.

There is more than this, however, to preconscious functions. Preconscious processes are not circumscribed by the more pedestrian and literal restrictions of conscious language. To these symbolic images which are based predominantly, although not exclusively, on exteroceptive stimuli, preconscious processes add another type of sensory imagery which has its major roots both in entero- and proprioceptive experiences.* These approximate less closely the limited one-to-one relationships of the fully matured language of conscious symbolic functions, but retain a broader overlapping base of multiple meanings. This enables them to use the symbolic process in a more allegorical and figurative fashion. In the adult who is not hamstrung by conscious or unconscious fear and guilt, preconscious processes make free use of analogy and allegory, superimposing dissimilar ingredients into new perceptual and conceptual patterns, thus reshuffling experience to achieve that fantastic degree of condensation without which creativity in any field of activity would be impossible. In the preconscious use of imagery and allegory many experiences are condensed into a single hieroglyph, which expresses in one symbol far more than one can say slowly and precisely, word by word, on the fully conscious level. This is why preconscious mentation is

* See Appendix

34

the Seven-league Boot of intuitive creative functions. This is how and why preconscious condensations are used in poetry, humor, the dream, and the symptom. Preconscious processes also play a vital role in the condensations of the mathematical symbol; which in other ways and at the same time resembles a special type of highly differentiated and specialized speech. The relation of the preconscious contribution to that made by the Unconscious System will be discussed below.

I hope that a picture is gradually emerging of the extraordinary importance of preconscious functions both as the great economizer, and as our automatic creative implement, that aspect of human mental processes which makes the difference between an adding machine and an electronic computer. For, like the electronic computer, the Preconscious System can be the direct recipient and utilizer of informational data without requiring the slower-paced interposition of conscious processes.

An example is the phenomenon of so-called hypermnesia under hypnosis.[4] In this experiment a subject will be brought into a strange room for a few minutes. When asked subsequently to list every item that he has seen, he will reproduce twenty or thirty items. Thereupon under hypnosis he will go on to reproduce another two hundred items. All of this indicates how much intake, registering, recording, and recalling can occur without participation of conscious awareness at any step in the process. It follows that there must be an incessant bombardment with preconscious stimuli all day long in every life and

---

[4] A capacity for immediate registration and precise recall of many more individual items than is possible under ordinary circumstances.

probably in reduced amounts at night as well, guiding the flow of our associations, of our moods, and of our autonomic reactions.

A beginning has been made of a more precise experimental investigation of this process by the tachistoscopic investigations of Fisher (14), of Lindley (56), and of Marsh and Worden (61).* These add greatly to our understanding of preconscious functions. They suggest that it may be the *speed* of a process and/or the duration or density (i.e., rate of repetition) which may determine whether it will operate preconsciously alone, or whether it will receive symbolic representation at all, and whether that symbolic representation will be on conscious or unconscious levels (55).

Here the relevant point is that the tachistoscopic experiments show how nearly instantaneously and without participation of conscious processes we can record visual, auditory, and proprioceptive experiences, sort them under the influence of affective weighting, route them directly to autonomic responses, and represent them later in such behavioral responses as "doodling," or in the visual imagery of dreams, sometimes in disguised and sometimes in transparent forms. These investigations make it clear that from the earliest years of human life all sensory modalities transmit a continuous bombardment of afferent impulses which may remain preconscious, yet influence all levels of response. They may, for example, touch off isolated and fragmentary patterns, or such complex patterns as the shaping of personality and the child's automatic imitation of adult postures and intonations, or the way faces and voices and handwritings of men and women may grow to look alike after years of close association.

It will be important to ascertain whether and to what extent and in what ways there are critical variations among human beings with respect to thresholds of preconscious perceptions of each of the sensory modalities, and also with respect to thresholds of symbolic and of autonomic responses to preconscious percepts. Do painters, sculptors, musicians, dancers, athletes, writers, dramatists, poets, mathematicians, and scientists show demonstrable differences in their constitutional or acquired equipment for preconscious function? How can these thresholds to preconscious afferents and the freedom of preconscious responses be influenced either favorably or unfavorably by conventional or new and hitherto undeveloped educational techniques?

There are active preconscious processes which have never been conscious, and preconscious processes which have been conscious during the learning period, but which are rendered preconscious through repetitive trials that lead to the acquisition of economizing, synergistic, goal-triggered patterns. However they arise, preconscious processes can have the highest degree of freedom in allegory and in figurative imagination which is attainable by any psychological process. The contribution of preconscious processes to creativity depends upon their freedom in gathering, assembling, comparing, and reshuffling of ideas. Indeed the special creative virtue of this continuous play of preconscious processes, concurrently with conscious and unconscious processes, lies in the fact that it is the preconscious type of symbolic function which frees our psychic apparatus (and more specifically our

37

symbolic processes) from rigidity. Where conscious processes predominate at one end of the spectrum, rigidity is imposed by the fact that conscious symbolic functions are anchored by their precise and literal relationships to specific conceptual and perceptual units. Where unconscious processes predominate at the other end of the spectrum there is an even more rigid anchorage, but in this instance to unreality: that is, to those unacceptable conflicts, objects, aims, and impulses which have been rendered inaccessible both to conscious introspection and to the corrective influence of experience, and which are represented by their own special symbols in impenetrable and fixed disguises. As long as their roots remain unconscious, the symbolic representative will remain unmodifiable. This is what renders them rigid.

Yet flexibility of symbolic imagery is essential if the symbolic process is to have that creative potential which is our supreme human trait. I will repeat that this creative flexibility is made possible predominantly if not exclusively by the free, continuous, and concurrent action of preconscious processes. As long as preconscious processes function freely, no scientist and no artist need fear that to sacrifice the unhappy luxury of being neurotic will leave his creative powers paralyzed. Quite on the contrary, if he emerges from the tyrannical and rigidly stereotyped domination of his own unconscious processes, his creative potential will be freer both quantitatively and qualitatively. I emphasize this because so many artists, so many writers, and so many scientists as well, are literally terrified of getting well. They have a strange and defensive fear that if they give up their neuroses they will cease to be creative, not realizing that to escape enslavement to their own unconscious will free their preconscious creative potential. Moreover, no matter how thoroughly analyzed they may be, they need not fear that in reality they will ever come up without a salty seasoning of unconscious propulsions. These they can use as the chestnut burr under the saddle, as a supplement to, but not as a substitute for, the powerful driving of the broncho's hind legs, which are the more fundamental, biogenetic, and instinctual processes, guided and supplemented by conscious and preconscious appetites and purposes. The rigid anchorage at both ends of the spectrum which is shown in the next diagrams is what frustrates and limits the creative process. Domination by the Unconscious end is what imposes rigidly repetitive idiosyncratic distortions upon Man's creative potential. I have tried to represent this diagrammatically in Fig. 4.

Manifestations of Preconscious Function

The free play of preconscious processes accomplishes two goals concurrently: it supplies an endless stream of old data rearranged into new combinations of wholes and fragments on grounds of analogic elements; and it exercises a continuous selective influence not only on free associations, but also on the minutiae of living, thinking, walking, talking, dreaming, and indeed of every moment of life. Let me give two very simple examples:

(1) A man had been deeply hurt by a girl with whom he had planned to go off for a weekend's visit to the distant home of mutual friends. He wanted both to talk about it and not to talk about it. So he reported the event in these words: "We left at eight o'clock." Unwittingly

39

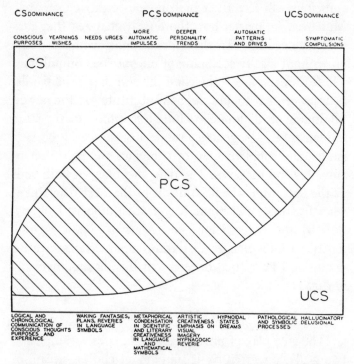

FIG. 4. Figures 1 and 3 were purposefully simplified by omitting PCS functions. The figure above represents hypothetical relationships somewhat crudely but attempts to indicate something of their complexities. The shapes of the curves, their points of origin and insertion, the areas they subtend are all hypothetical. Even the implied assumption that their interrelationships can be expressed in quantitative terms is only a working hypothesis. Therefore the diagram is not to be taken literally. It is designed rather to illustrate complex interrelationships, as they may be assumed to occur in nature (i.e., human nature), in which the concurrent action of preconscious processes frees our psychic apparatus, and more specifically our symbolic processes, from rigid anchorage. At the conscious end of the diagram this anchorage is to fixed and literal relationships to external realities. At the unconscious end of the diagram, there is if anything an even more rigid anchorage to unreality, because the unconscious symbolic relationships which dominate at this end of the spectrum are unmodifiable by experience as long as they remain unconscious. The flexible and creative contribution made to our psychic processes by the concurrent play of preconscious processes is illustrated in the middle band.

he had omitted to indicate whether he meant eight in the morning or eight in the evening, and thus obscured the issue of how and where they were going to spend that night. This spared him the pain of going into the details of his failure with her. Later, when he had to describe how the girl was constantly looking over her shoulder at other men, he said, "She went out looking for some *person*." Again without realizing it he had chosen the ambiguous word "person," which would spare him the pain of stating clearly whether she had been looking for a friend, a couple, a girl, or another man.

(2) In tracing a path between the laboratory and her home a woman scientist automatically found herself choosing a certain sequence of streets and turns rather than its mirror image. The two paths were precisely the same in distance. There was nothing to choose between them with respect to the pleasantness or unpleasantness of the walk. But she had a strong preference for one over the other. As she allowed her thoughts to roam more freely than her steps, it became clear to her that one route traced a letter which was the first letter in the name of the person who was the major source of pain in her life, a fact which she did not want to face openly. She did not want to acknowledge that she knew that her husband was a homosexual, and she did not want to trace the letter with which the name of his "boy friend" began. As her feet traversed the streets on her daily path, an automatic Preconscious, but not Unconscious process, chose her path for her.

Preconscious functions can also express themselves in a free fashion in the choice of gifts. A woman who was involved in a bitter matrimonial battle made an effort to heal the rift at Christmas time by giving her husband a brace of antique dueling pistols. She wanted to be rid of him even as she made amends. Nor should we overlook the concurrent unconscious guilty suicidal implication of the fact that he was a dead-shot, while she had never shot a gun of any kind. Could any formal work of art say more in fewer words?

Another woman, an artist, painted a series of individual Christmas cards, each of which was for her a single flashing image out of a dream. She painted only at night; and she painted swiftly in a state of intense concentration and abstraction. To a matriarchal and spinsterish mother she gave an Archangel; the Annunciation to a brother-in-law who was a notorious woman-chaser. With her tongue firmly planted in her cheek she painted the Virgin and Child for an Amazonian sister; and she painted a sad and clownlike self-portrait for her analyst. She did not plan any of these gifts. Yet as she finished each painting, with a subtle mixture of compassion and unconscious irony she knew at once for whom it was intended. In another dream some months later, a cyclopean, one-eyed clown, with a whitewashed and blinded eye-socket, appeared in the role of the analyst to complement the latent meanings of her painting.

One can trace the same play of preconscious functions in handwriting, in design patterns, in automatic drawing, in writing and doodling. This has been shown experimentally under hypnosis (33). It can be observed in the production of the voice and its pitch, in posture and the manner in which we walk, in condensed and repetitive turns of phrase, and also in the modes of art and music. One writer disembodies literature by turning words into musical notes. One musician uses music as a way of maintaining a safe distance between him and his audience. For another it is an instrument with which he smashes in the heads of his listeners. A huge man always walks on tiptoe and talks in a whispered falsetto when he is consumed with rage.

A man of enormous creative capacity has rarely been able to complete any work because he never could free his preconscious functions from imprisonment by unconscious rage and terror. Because of this he has remained a frustrated if acute reporter and critic, but never a creator. His inability to produce free associations either on the analytic couch or in his own work was the measure of his inability to exercise freely his preconscious functions. By his blind terror of abandoning himself to his own preconscious he was anchored to reality at one end, and to a dreamlike fixity of unconscious symbols at the other.

I have checked my records and it turns out that I have never had a patient who could not produce free associations yet could drive a car with confidence. I have had a few patients who could not produce free associations yet could drive a car only forward (usually with intermittent anxiety) but were unable to back their cars or to park them.

I have chosen a mixed bag of elementary examples to illustrate how the creative process depends for its freedom upon the play of those preconscious functions which are balanced precariously between the rigidity of conscious function at one end (with its anchorage in reality), and the rigidity of unconscious function at the other end (with its anchorage in the stereotyped and repetitive symbolism of unconscious processes). It is a measure of the profound and tragic failure of our educational process that it does not accept the challenge of this problem, but tends if anything to reinforce the imprisonment of preconscious function. (This will be discussed in the final chapter.)

Let me recapitulate briefly this essential element in my story. Conscious anchorage to reality is, as we have already seen, chronological and logical. It is rooted in conscious representations of perceptions which are built out of exteroceptive, proprioceptive, and enteroceptive units. Of these the exteroceptive perceptions are readily checked and controlled because we can compare them, and when desirable, in some measure shut them out. The proprioceptive contributions come next. Internal perceptions are the most difficult modalities to control, compare, and interrupt. In turn this is why the three perceptual fields play different roles in fantasies, symptoms, and dreams (27).

At the other pole (i.e., of "unconscious" symbolism) the symbolic process never represents current perceptual processes, but only memory traces of a past to which it is unalterably and rigidly anchored. Specifically this is because of the iron curtain which separates the "unconscious" symbol from that which it both represents and disguises. As long as that iron curtain separates the two, their relationship to each other cannot be altered either by experience or by imagination. It is for this reason that the symbolic process at the "unconscious" end of the spectrum is sterile, repetitive, non-creative, and incapable of communicating even its limited stocks of meanings.

In between come the preconscious functions with their automatic and subtle recordings of multiple perceptions, their automatic recall, their multiple analogic and overlapping linkages, and their direct connections to the autonomic processes which underlie affective states. The rich play of preconscious operations occurs freely in states of abstraction, in sleep, in dreams, and as we write, paint, or allow our thoughts to flow in the non-selected paths of free association.

Preconscious processes are assailed from both sides. From one side they are nagged and prodded into rigid and distorted symbols by unconscious drives which are oriented away from reality and which consist of rigid compromise formations, lacking in fluid inventiveness. From the other side they are driven by literal conscious purpose, checked and corrected by conscious retrospective critique. The uniqueness of creativity, i.e., its capacity to find and put together something new, depends on the extent to which preconscious functions can operate freely between these two ubiquitous concurrent and oppressive prison wardens.

A Brief Excursion into Psychoanalytic Theory concerning Preconscious Processes

In placing a major emphasis on the creative role not of unconscious or of conscious but of preconscious processes, I am departing from the older classical analytic thought about this problem. A few more recent contributors have begun to move in this same direction. Among these the late Ernst Kris was outstanding (28). In chapter XV of his book, Kris touches on the development of Freud's concept of the preconscious and its changing uses, and the varied ways in which the concept has been used by other psychoanalytic writers. He notes in passing how inadequate has been the consideration of this component in mental processes and then indicates that most users of it have implied that in one way or another it was a way-station between conscious and unconscious processes, that some writers attribute some degree of verbalization to it which others withhold, that some relate it more closely to ego functions than do others. Kris himself relates it in varying ways to the obliteration or withdrawal of cathexes. These varying formulations differ from the conception which I am advancing here.

It would require the dedicated zeal of an anthropologist and the full-time activity of a team of research workers to trace through the ramifications of psychoanalytic literature the origin and development of the idea that it is the unconscious aspect of man's psychological processes which is the source of his creative inspiration, his creative zeal, of his creative uniqueness. Such a search would have to include an historical survey of the development of many bypaths, such as the work of Rank, Jung, Adler, Horney and her followers, Harry Stack Sullivan, and Melanie Klein.

This would be in addition to tracing the same theme through the work of those, who, rightly or wrongly, kept closer to the main development line of psychoanalytic theory. Here we have in mind the original studies of Freud on Leonardo da Vinci (16), Dostoevsky (18), Gradiva (17), the early studies of Ferenczi, of Ernest Jones (27), and of Theodore Reik, plus the many studies by individual analysts of individual works of art which one finds throughout the course of psychoanalytic writing down to and including the recent studies by Phyllis

Greenacre (21) of Dean Swift and Lewis Carroll. Set squarely in the midst of these were the writings by Hanns Sachs which were collected under the title *The Creative Unconscious* (71).

It is not my purpose here to attempt to survey this literature. To do so would be of value and interest in a history of the development of psychoanalytic thought; but it is not germane to my central theme. Moreover, most of this material would have to be reformulated to-day in terms of recent developments in psychoanalytic theory, including some which are still emergent and whose advent was implicit if not fully explicit in the emphasis placed by Ernst Kris, not on the role of *unconscious processes* in the creative act, but on that aspect of mentation which Freud called the *System Preconscious*.

Earlier studies of creativity had in common a recognition of the fact that, although conscious processes played an important role in the final shaping of the form of the creative product, the roots of creativity lie in deeper and more obscure processes which work with a speed far greater than can be achieved by that fragment of our psychological processes of which we are conscious. In early days the importance of the unconscious in the derivation and shaping of the neurotic process was still a fresh and astonishing discovery. Therefore it was natural to assume that it must also be the source of the creative drive and of the great creative inspiration in human life. It is out of this natural but fallacious deduction that many erroneous clichés have been drawn: such as the notion that a man produces only from his unconscious, that to be creative a man must be sick, and that consequently the artist, scientist, or writer had better guard and protect his

47

neurosis from the therapeutic intervention of the psychiatrist. Indeed in the minds of many it has placed the psychiatrist in the role of the obsessionally tidy housewife, who makes it impossible for anyone to live in a home lest anything get out of place or lest any dust accumulate under the rug.

The further fact that many creative people, whether in the arts or in science, or in other fields of life, have in truth been psychologically ill, has led to the easy but fallacious assumption that the coincidence of creativity and neurosis implied a direct necessary and causal relationship between them.

Common to most earlier writings on the topic, and obscuring and beclouding their formulations, is a confusion between unconscious and preconscious functions. Thus when Sachs speaks of "toying with the unconscious" he is dealing really with preconscious functions as these are warped by the pressure of unconscious processes. If out of this interaction any creativity survives, this is due primarily and preponderantly to preconscious and not unconscious processes.

Similar examples could be drawn from most of the early literature on this topic; but I believe that it would come closer to the truth, or at least closer to the thesis which I am presenting here, to say that the creative person is one who in some manner, which today is still accidental, has retained his capacity to use his preconscious functions more freely than is true of others who may potentially be equally gifted. The preconscious functions operate constantly between the imprisoning and restricting influences of conscious and unconscious processes; and the creative future of humanity depends on the successful working out of the interrelationship among these three facets of human psychological experience.

Perhaps one of the most extraordinary examples of both the perceptual and freely creative functioning of preconscious processes is seen in the behavior of a great mathematician who can sleep snoring in the midst of a heated debate, and erupt out of the middle of a snore to participate appropriately in the middle of the debate which has been going on around him. That his preconscious processes of perception and of ratiocination have continued at top speed even in sleep is demonstrated almost experimentally in such repeated experiences.

Another impressive example is to be found in studies of Form as they occur in nature. Although not dealing directly with the creative process, the contributors to a volume edited by L. L. Whyte (77) cover a range of human interests and activities which include crystallography, astronomy, animal genetics, plant physiology, chemistry, human anatomy and embryology, comparative psychology and ethology, neuro-physiology, psychology, the history of fine arts, and gestalt psychology. All deal with the processes which determine form in nature and relate it to form in creativity. The material is relevant to my thesis insofar as I assume the existence of an incessant bombardment of the human psychological apparatus by preconscious influences which give shape to our thoughts, feelings, and purposes, independently of conscious or unconscious factors. These then are projected in time and space, in dream and word, in painting and sculpture, in sound and music, and in abstract conceptualizations. The extraordinary parallels which exist among the forms assumed by the productions of nature and of

49

man can best be understood in terms of some such theory as this: i.e., that the impact on human beings of the forms and patterns which play upon our preconscious perceptual processes incessantly from earliest infancy to old age shapes our creative responses without our knowledge.

6. CREATIVITY

It is, I believe, a fair generalization to state quite simply that although the uncovering of new facts and of new relationships among both new and old data is not the whole of creativity, it is the essential process without which there can be no such thing as creativity. Consequently creativity implies *invention* (Nicole, 66): e.g., the making of new machines or processes by the application of old or new facts and principles or a combination of them in order to uncover still newer facts and newer combinations, and to synthesize new patterns out of data whose interdependence had hitherto gone unnoted and unused. It is this which is common to all creativeness, whether in music as described by Mozart, or in painting as described by Delacroix and others, or in poetry as described by Paul Valéry, A. E. Housman, etc., or in science as pointed out by Gregg (22), Claude Bernard (3), Richard Tolman (75), Richet (70), and other scientists.

It is of some historical and linguistic interest, as Hadamard (23) indicates (p. 29), that according to Max Muller "cogito" originally meant "to shake together"; whereas "intelligo," according to St. Augustine, meant "to select from among." Cogitation and intelligence: "Cogito" to shake things up, to roll the bones of one's ideas, memories and feelings, to make a great melting-pot of experience: plus the superimposed process of *"intelligo"*: i.e., consciously, self-critically but retrospectively, an after-the-act process of choosing from among unanticipated combinations those patterns which have new significance. In the arts the process characterized by St. Augustine as *"intelligo"* tests the creative products for

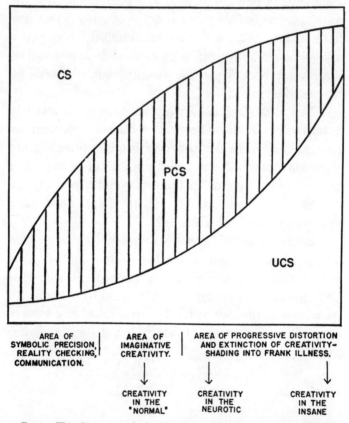

AREA OF SYMBOLIC PRECISION, REALITY CHECKING, COMMUNICATION.	AREA OF IMAGINATIVE CREATIVITY.	AREA OF PROGRESSIVE DISTORTION AND EXTINCTION OF CREATIVITY— SHADING INTO FRANK ILLNESS.
↓	↓	↓
CREATIVITY IN THE "NORMAL"	CREATIVITY IN THE NEUROTIC	CREATIVITY IN THE INSANE

FIG. 5. This figure extends further the implications of the diagrammatic representation of the interrelationships among the three systems. It is an attempt to show at least one way in which the variations in their relative roles may explain the distortions of creativity under the impact of neurotogenic UCS processes.

their communicability both as intellectual and as emotional experiences. In science *"intelligo"* tests them for their validity. In psychoanalysis we try to test them for both, which accounts in part for the special position of psychoanalysis as a bridge between science and the arts.

We have seen that the *"cogito"* component, i.e., the assembling of new combinations, is predominantly a *preconscious* process and *not* a product of unconscious processes as is so often said; whereas *"intelligo"* is of necessity preponderantly *conscious* (although here too preconscious processes play an essential contributory and economizing role).

The special vulnerability of preconscious processes to distortion under the influences of unconscious neurotogenic forces will be contrasted with the creative alliance of preconscious with conscious processes of retrospective critique and evaluation in those rare and happy circumstances when these can operate free from interference from unconscious processes.

Starting from this as a working hypothesis, our next step is an observation which has been made by many writers, scientists, artists, and musicians—namely, that new combinations are rarely if ever found by straining for them consciously, but rather by a process of free association, with a discussion of which I will open the next chapter.

Chapter 2
The Interactions between Creative and Neurotogenic Processes

1. THE EXPLORATORY AND CREATIVE FUNCTIONS OF FREE ASSOCIATIONS

Free associations have a general significance beyond their exploratory importance in psychoanalytic technique. It is through free associations that the mind shakes itself out of its ruts, or if you prefer Max Müller's figure (23) shakes itself apart and together again, finding its way off the beaten path, stumbling onto new connections. It is through free association that the mind moves without conscious, deliberate bias or preconception from thought to thought, from idea to idea, from feeling to feeling. Where it is not subjected to distorting pressures from unconscious processes, it is the most spontaneous, primitive, natural, and creative process of thought. Moreover it is as direct an expression of one of the two vital functions of the preconscious system in action as we can achieve.

Yet it is not always realized that free association is the natural process by which man creates, whether he is an artist, scientist, lawyer, businessman, analyst, or analysand. By means of free associations the psychological processes roam freely from mental highways to its byways, unhampered by conscious restrictions, gathering analogous but seemingly unrelated ideas and impressions, putting them together in varying combinations until new relationships and new patterns come into view. Both in

53

science and in the arts, free association is the essential instrument in the process of creative search. It is the process of "*cogito*," i.e., of "shaking together."

Subsequently the new patterns must be subjected to a process of retrospective, conscious, self-critical scrutiny for a necessary secondary process of checking and testing. This is "*intelligo*," the "selection from among many." In the psychoanalytic process, especially at first, "*cogito*" is done mainly by the patient, whereas "*intelligo*" is done by the analyst almost alone. Later in the analysis this may be done by the analyst and patient together. In the work of the creative artist or scientist, both "*cogito*" and "*intelligo*" must from the first be done by one individual, working more or less alone. The first step is carried out, for the most part, preconsciously, the second, for the most part, consciously. If we bear in mind the fact that the creative process requires this flexible alternation of roles, its vulnerability will become clear.

There is an important analogy between the creative process in the sciences and the arts and the processes of free association: an analogy which is so close as to be almost an identity. This arises from the fact that it is impossible to produce free associations, to be freely imaginative, to be freely creative if at the same time and in the very moment of "freedom" one attempts to maintain a watchful, critical scrutiny of what one is producing. The person who is producing free associations with least internal friction and interference is unable subsequently to retrace the path of his associations, unable usually to remember many of the items or their sequence. (This is analogous to the difficulty one has in recalling a list of nonsense syllables, which, rearranged to form words and

54

sentences, would be easily remembered as a single
Therefore any retrospective inspection of free assoc.
must depend upon a detached observer who notes and
records their sequence, or upon some automatic recording device. Similarly, the creative scientist or the creative
artist, writer, or musician, has to set down his productions, put them aside, and let time elapse, before he will
be able to turn back to them with objective scrutiny, with
lessened identification and less personalized defense of
them, than is possible at the moment of creating or immediately thereafter. This ability to get outside of one's
own skin, to view one's own productions as though one
were a third person, involves a transition from preconscious symbolic functions and preconscious identifications
to conscious and objective self-criticism. At the same time
it requires a purging of conscious and preconscious processes of the unconscious ax-grinding which arises out of
deeper levels of conflict and pain. (Examples of this
struggle will be found in the subsequent sections.)

There are several further facts about the process of
free association which are relevant to our problem:

(1) The technique of free association has a basis in
well-established facts of neurophysiology. As indicated
elsewhere (43, 55), free associations are the obverse of the
conditioned reflex. The conditioned reflex depends upon
the fact that within any limited period of time no two
experiences can impinge on the nervous system without
setting up a connecting link, the nature of which is dependent in part on the time interval between the two.
Obversely, free associations depend upon the fact that
actions, thoughts, ideas, and feelings which emerge from

the nervous system in any time-bound fashion must also have a meaningful interrelationship.

(2) Furthermore, the technique and process of free association is an effort-free scanning device, comparable in speed to the scanning operations of television or of the electronic computer. This is relevant to all comparisons of the creative operations of preconscious functions to the operations of electronic machines (55).

(3) In psychological affairs, free associations are our Gallup Poll. As already indicated, speech is a pedestrian and highly selective process which produces weighted samples of the mind's activities. Free associations constitute a technique for securing an approximation to a representative sampling of all that is going on in the mind at any one time. Furthermore, it is the only technique by which we can minimize the weighting of the sampling process that occurs automatically during ordinary processes of communication. We convey a meaning by deliberately and consciously choosing a topic to talk about. This results in a preconscious selection of related items, with a concomitant rejection of irrelevant and intrusive thoughts. This has two consequences. It places the emphasis on logical rather than analogical relationships, thus impeding any creative discovery of new relationships; and it wholly masks the concurrent influence on the stream of associations which is exercised by unconscious processes.

(4) The word "free" does not imply here any exemption from causal sequences. Nor is there any implication of the mystical or supernatural. This is not what "free" means in reference to "free associations." It implies rather two kinds or degrees of freedom:

56

Freedom from conscious and deliberate interference with the spontaneous stream of thought and feeling, as nearly as human purpose can achieve this. When we allow our thoughts to follow their own bent, we do not choose ahead of time to think or talk about any topic nor to adhere to any one topic which comes to mind. Nor do we determine *not* to think or talk about anything. All conscious, voluntary screening is thus reduced to a minimum.

This makes possible an even more significant degree of freedom. As already described, the choice of any topic for discussion sets in motion automatic preconscious processes of selection and rejection from among all possible elements in the stream of association. Contrariwise, whenever we allow our thoughts to roam without a preselected goal, this process of automatic preconscious selecting and rejecting remains relatively inactive, exposing (a) the influences arising from *unconscious* fear, guilt, hate, purpose, and conflict; (b) those influences which are dependent upon analogic relationships in the associative stream (from which all creativity derives); and (c) those which emanate from concurrent physiological variables.

Consequently, creativity itself depends upon the process of free association, which makes possible preconscious analogic processes, yet at the same time exposes them to deformation under the influence of concurrent unconscious processes. This inescapable paradox lies close to the heart of our problem. Free associations are essential to creativity; because they free the sensitive, fluid, and plastic preconscious system from the rigidity imposed at the conscious end of the symbolic spectrum. Yet at the same time they expose it to the distortions and also to the rigidity imposed by the unconscious system.

This conflicting confluence of forceful influences occurs under two circumstances: (a) It is used deliberately and for therapeutic purposes in analysis to expose the distorting influence of unconscious processes. (b) It occurs in spontaneous or induced states of partial dissociation, as in falling asleep or waking, in hypnagogic reveries, under hypnosis or drugs, in states of abstraction or trance, or in those states of extreme concentration of attention which approach the process of hypnotic induction, and in which much scientific and artistic, literary, or musical creativity occurs.

I have said that free associations are the most natural and spontaneously creative process of which the mind is capable. Yet it would be quite fallacious to conclude from this that they are also the easiest. There are individuals for whom the process is impossible, except where they are entirely off guard, as when dozing, falling asleep, waking, under drugs, or delirious. These are individuals for whom this mental leap-in-the-dark is so fraught with guilt or terror that they can no more allow their thoughts to roam freely than they could run down a flight of stairs with closed eyes. Such individuals have to stretch out their mental toes to feel carefully for each next step before they can trust themselves to express a next word. Logical and chronological sequences are the hand-rail to which they always cling. For some people this is true even when they are alone. For others it is true only when in the presence of other human beings. Still others are hampered in this way when in the presence of certain people, but not of others. Actually for everyone, although in varying degrees, free associations carry implications of guilt or danger.

Nor is anxiety the only emotion which can limit the exercise of this freely searching, scanning, seeking, shaking-together process, which we call "free association." Even those who are able to let down their guard for a time may suddenly find that their unguided stream of thought and feeling has carried them over uncharted seas to unanticipated shores, inhabited by strange impulses and ideas. Their somnolent inattention to where they are going will suddenly be punctuated by jets of guilt, terror, or rage. This occurs to many people on dropping off to sleep. The brief cat-nap which is interrupted by a sudden involuntary jerk is a familiar example of this.

It is clear, therefore, that the influence of painful emotions on all levels, unconscious, preconscious, as well as conscious, plays a significant role in determining the freedom with which even the most brilliantly equipped mind can function in creative work. Any artist or scientist may be guilt-free, hate-free, and anxiety-free in certain directions, yet hampered by any or all of these affects in other areas. As a result this individual may function with free creative energy in some fields, yet be wholly muscle-bound in others. Thus, objective tests showed that a young woman of exceptional general intellectual gifts also had the highest native mathematical aptitudes. Yet she was unable to perform even the simplest mathematical process; because mathematics was forbidden to her by unconscious taboos arising out of the fact that to her they represented the forbidden territory of a man's life and a man's body. Comparable examples are familiar to all of us.

There is partial evidence which suggests that where interfering affects operate predominantly on an unconscious level, their influence tends to spread so as to exercise a diffusely inhibitory effect, blocking the flow of all freely creative associations. When, on the other hand, they operate on a preponderantly preconscious level, their influence will be more selective, with the result that they will be inhibitory in certain directions and overdriving in other compensatory areas. The evidence for this is not conclusive; but it is a clue which is worth exploring in our effort to understand the difference between those who become paralyzed by anxiety and those who are spurred on by it; and also to understand how in certain individuals anxiety itself can give rise to an irresistible pressure to produce warped artistic or scientific creations.

As already mentioned, there are affects other than anxiety which hamper and limit and restrict and even paralyze the inherent capacity of the mind to produce free associations. Guilt and shame, whether conscious or masked, are important here as well as rage and hatred. Everything which has been said about anxiety applies to these other affective attitudes as well.

Before bringing this portion of our discussion to a close, it is well to emphasize that out of the algebraic summation of these many processes come positive as well as negative forces. The mind is an instrument that grinds its axes unconsciously more often than consciously: trying to prove points that it has to prove, and not hesitating to strain the truth in the effort to achieve this goal. In other words, unconscious conflicts and necessities which are carried over from the nursery, from childhood, and from schooling, reappear in many disguised forms throughout life. They may be expressed in an effort to disprove something which is true; or conversely they may drive a man to attempt to prove the impossible. Or they may drive the creative zeal blindly in an effort to resolve some ancient dilemma, to pay an old debt or to settle an old grudge, to achieve the unattainable goal of a childhood fantasy, or to lift the curse from something which in childhood had been an overwhelming source of pain, humiliation, and terror. Such is the quality of the rational yet irrational, unattainable yet necessary and unconscious purposes which warp and restrict the processes of free association. All such forces as these, if they are truly unconscious, operate below the surface to distort the freer analogic links in the chain of free associations. They come to clear expression only when conscious selection and rejection can be put aside, with a concurrent reduction of preconscious screening, or in such states of dissociated consciousness as occur in dreams, in sleep, under medication, in deliria, in hypnagogic reveries, in hypnosis, in illness, and in the automatic creative experiences which have been described by many poets and writers as well as scientists.

This point is essential, because it highlights the difference between the freely creative interplay among preconscious and conscious processes, which facilitates the production of free associations when unconscious processes do not play a disproportionate role; in contrast to the warped distortion of the creative process which occurs whenever unconscious processes gain the preponderant position among these three concurrent systems of psychological processes.

2. DISTORTIONS ARISING THROUGH THE SHIFT OF DOMINANCE OVER THE PRECONSCIOUS FROM CONSCIOUS TO UNCONSCIOUS PROCESSES

It is not possible to characterize fully or with precision all of the differences between the modes of function of preconscious processes in ordinary speech and in creative activity. It is possible, however, to pick out certain essential differences. As already described, in communication the major function of preconscious processes is to carry out nearly instantaneous, effortless, and automatic rejection of irrelevancies and the selection of those items which cluster around the pre-selected goal. In creative activity, on the other hand, the function of preconscious processes is the equally automatic and effortless assembling of fragmentary items into new constellations on the basis of analogic characteristics.

Both processes are vulnerable to distortion under the impact of unconscious forces. In communication this is manifested in the well-known examples of slips of the tongue, of the pen, and of the ear. In creativity the impact is more subtle and complex, showing itself primarily in the crippling of the capacity to assemble new data or to arrange old data in new patterns. This is the result of a tendency which arises whenever unconscious processes play a dominant role, and which consequently characterizes all neurotic disturbances whatever their nature, namely to develop stereotyped and rigid repetitiveness.

Innumerable examples of this could be given from all of the arts, e.g., from painting, from the work of playwrights, from the work of poets, the work of dancers and composers. In paintings this stereotype may be evident for years in the works of men of world-wide reputations; who after passing through some inner convulsion of the spirit, start on a new "period," dominated perhaps by a new color, or by new subject matter, or by a new way of applying the paint, or a new way of stressing the outline, or a new way of distorting proportions. Yet each such innovation soon reveals the same rigidity as the old; and often the same unconscious preoccupations can be recognized beneath the new costume. This is evident to anyone who has studied an historical review of Picasso.

A playwright may write half a dozen plays which portray the same theme in various disguises, e.g., a father's struggle to mask his destructive homosexual impulses toward his sons. This theme will be expressed in a series of disguises, without resolution, and with a mounting frustration which colors each successive version. Yet it may remain so well masked that the audience and critics can no more understand the play than they can understand those neurotic symptoms which assume more banal and everyday forms. Therefore from such art, no matter how artful, no one gains: not the playwright, the players, or the audience. All that triumphs is the impenetrable and insistent rigidity which betrays the failure of art to resolve the neurotic components of the artist and of the culture from which he springs. The neurotic in art is no more self-healing than is the neurotic in the clinic.

Or a dancer may hang the arms as though they were legs, and flail the legs like arms, all the while backing her way into every line of choreographic movement bent over and buttocks first, with tiny little festinating steps like children playing choo-choo trains backwards; and the content of her dances may betray an inversion of all sexual roles. This may be repeated in a long series of dances over a period of years. Insemination rites are danced in which the men are women and the women men. Or if, as sometimes happens, women are allowed to dance the woman's part, they mock the feminine by simpering posture and gesture as they dance, to the accompaniment of delighted cackles of homosexual laughter in the self-selected audience of balletomanes. Here again most striking is the fact that no matter how skillful the craftsmanship, this is an essentially non-creative, sterile, and rigid stereotype, with no forward movement of mind or spirit on the part of choreographers, dancers, or audience.

In music there can be the same enslavement of the composer's preconscious creative faculties by his own unconscious processes, which limit the free scope of his preconscious inventiveness, cramp his musical imagination into a sterile and rigid model, force him to be repetitious—and often make it impossible to stop when he has said all that he has to say. Such composers, who include some of the greatest, are like the departing guest who cannot bring himself to leave because of a compulsive necessity to find just one more magical phrase.

If then we keep our eyes on the fact that the essence of the neurotic process is that there are forces at work which predetermine the automatic repetition of any form of behavior or its equally automatic extinction, one sees this betraying itself in a tragic fashion in the work even of the most gifted. This accounts not only for the personal sterility and impotence of great artists, writers, musicians, and scientists, but also for the cultural sterility and impotence of great art and literature, music, and science.

This thesis is so pregnant with devastating implications that it merits careful thought on the part of anyone who hopes to turn culture into a more effective instrument for the evolution of the human spirit. Certainly one must admit that if the system of unconscious symbolic processes does in fact play the destructive role in relation to creativity which I attribute to it, reducing man's enormous creative potential to a sterile impotent monotone, then to imagine that the unconscious is the source of creativity becomes a tragic perversion and mockery of every high human aspiration.

We learn most from that which is the furthest from the norm. We learn from the autopsy table the lessons that ultimately make it possible to prevent the disease which produced the death. So we learn from the extremes of illness the lessons which illuminate and ultimately safeguard the normal. This has been true in physiology; and it is proving to be true in psychology.

An example of this is seen in the work of a highly gifted but paranoid schizophrenic architect, which impressed everyone both with its brilliance and its incomprehensibility. The steady and inexorable pressure of his delusions ultimately forced his hospitalization. Finally in the treatment situation he said, "I must create a space which will be different in shape and dimensions from any space where I have ever been before, different from the space which I ultimately came from." These sick and poetic words give us at least a glimmering of understanding of why the brilliant productions of his genius were incomprehensible to anyone, including himself, and how his great preconscious instrument had been taken over by his unconscious and perverted to the uses of delusion. The next sections will provide further examples.

3. Examples from Dreams and Dreamlike States

(1) A patient presented me with a reverie which in an extraordinarily condensed way recapitulated with amazing precision a problem which was presented by another patient, a writer who lived it out not in a dream but in a book that she was writing. (I can give no details here without violating her privacy.)

For years the first patient had suffered at times from restless insomnia, during which his mind flooded with angry fragmentary notions. On one occasion, many years before he had come for treatment, one strange sentence had come to him as he lay and tossed. The sentence was, "*Hitler kills 43,000 Germans.*" Almost at once he had relaxed and fallen asleep. Subsequently he began to notice that whenever this sentence came to him during his bouts of insomnia, he would relax at once, and in a moment fall asleep. As this sentence emerged unsought, he would know that he was about to sleep and did so. Gradually over the years this became his regular automatic invocation to sleep.

This confronts us with a problem. Why does this sudden sentence acquire for him this idiosyncratic trigger value? His free associations made clear the play of preconscious and unconscious processes in its production. This patient is an anti-Semitic Jew. Hitler is the Jew-killer. Hitler is his own hired gunman, his Murder Incorporated. He feels safer in the world because so many Jews have been killed. He feels exultant. He dances a war dance with the victorious chant of savages after the kill. But his conscience makes it impossible for him to experience this great relief from saying "Hitler killed 6,000,-

ooo Jews." So 43,000 Germans are substituted for 6,000,-
ooo Jews. His conscience turns it into vengeance on
the German killers instead of the Jews. But why 43,000?
He recalls that at one time it used to be 80,000. Eighty
to him mean a ripe old age. In his childhood eighty-six
to ninety-six meant to him "as old as God." His mother
is in her eighties. His grandmother was German. He used
to love her and he used to serve her as her "page-boy." A
man in his forties is a foolish man. In 1943, in the
midst of the war about which he was in conflict, he broke
off relationships with a girl with whom he was more
deeply involved than anyone else in his life, a girl who
subsequently married a physician. With this girl on one
critical occasion he had attempted intercourse, had en-
tered and then had withdrawn saying, "I can't go through
with it." He had been 43 at the time. She was not a
Jewess. This had been his last "successful" affair. He had
actually dreamed of her the night before this fetishistic
sentence had first come to him, and again on the night
before he had mentioned it to me for the first time, although he had been in treatment for nearly two years.
The unconscious and preconscious sources of this psychopathological process are transparent. For several reasons I
will not try artificially to reconstruct here the entire story
of this symbolic trigger.

(2) Another example is of a dream which consisted
of the single word "twin," yet which condensed the entire tragic drama of a life. This single word was dreamed
by a man who had come to me for limited help of a specific nature. As colleagues we had also on occasion worked
together on another project. He was a man whose whole
life had been shattered by the forces of external circum-

stances. Consequently as an adult he found himself as much an outsider as he had been in childhood, when he had been a semi-invalid from polio, competing with a younger brother who was vigorous, tough, and larger. There had been a critical period in his relationship with his brother when it had looked as though only one of the two could survive a precarious situation. They had tossed coins for it. Ultimately both had escaped. This awful episode had remained a matter of deep horror to him for years.

During our work he had developed a sense of warm and close identification with me, so close indeed that on hearing me praised by a stranger at a dinner party, he had broken out with the word "thanks," as though the praise had been for himself. To become my twin, therefore, meant a new life with a new *identity* and new hopes, an escape from every old problem that he had ever had, almost a rebirth. At the same time, the word also carried unconscious homosexual implications which became clear as we worked along. And together with high aspirations went hidden fantasies of killing me and replacing me, as he had in fantasy often killed and replaced his brother. What work of art can achieve a condensation greater than this?

(3) Through no fault of his own and with pain, shortly after the death of the last remaining representative of the older generation of his own family, a man faced the dissolution of his own marriage. To this man sailing meant a great deal, and family ties meant everything. After recovering from the depression which the marital catastrophe had initially engendered, he was beginning to look both forward and backwards, with simul-

taneous pain and hope, and planned a short cruise. In this setting he dreamed that he came into port and dropped anchor in the late afternoon. Then he was walking towards shore along a dock, towards the top of which the tide was rising. As he neared the land a ramp descended into the water, so that a cold blue wave nearly submerged him as it rose to his shoulders. Everyone said to him, "Aren't you cold?" (His later thoughts were of the "douche of cold water" which his wife's attitude meant to him, of the rigidity which had chilled their sex life, and of his wife's cold blue eyes and dress as she had turned away from him.) In the dream he answered that he was not cold: and he felt proud of being able to plow on through, just as he had pushed through her cold blueness, without the protective armor which he himself could not wear as she did. Finally he reached shelter in an old house, where seated before the fire he found the aged relative who had just died and who had been almost a mother to him. She was in black, remote, silent, and unreal. In the dream he knew that she was dead. Nevertheless he could communicate with her; and he asked her lamely, "What is it like, where you were?" To this she made only some vaguely reassuring, noncommittal yet loving answer. With this benediction he felt comforted and he awakened.

(4) Out of a complex dream all that remained was the vivid image of a *Rabbit*. Associations led naturally and inevitably to bunnies in childhood, to the usual children's books, from Mollie Cottontail to Peter Rabbit and the ultimate triumph of the humble, to the disappearance and death of a pet rabbit, to the rabbit as the perpetually hunted animal, to false accusations of carelessness, to her

nickname in childhood, to the play *Harvey* (the rabbit that was not there), to the street name for the phallus she did not possess, to her impotent husband and her desire for children, to the rabbit as a symbol of procreation and fertility. One would look far to find in any art form a more complex or richer pattern of condensations.

(5) The brilliantly gifted painter, already mentioned above, produced a dream at a time in her life during which she had to manage several complex problems at once: those of her nearly psychotic husband, some complicated legal affairs, and several highly gifted children. She had been the youngest in her own family and had always been looked upon as an irresponsible, unruly, cantankerous person. In actuality, however, she had played a quite different role.

Her dream was that she is running, running, running in a desperate effort to move someone from one spot to another—a man who somehow or other was known yet unknown (the analyst). In the dream for some strange reason in order to achieve this (i.e., to get this figure some place in time) she had to paint him white, chalky-white, not the clown she painted so often, yet suggesting a clown; and it was especially the face, and especially around the eye or in the eye socket that she had to paint. Maybe the eye socket was empty—a single eye yet an unseeing eye. It was the kind of face that she liked well, although it was not identifiable. The age was unclear. And this was all she dreamed.

To this she quickly associated: a clown cleaning off his makeup or putting it on; a clown clowning; her own clowning at home, her role as court jester to keep everybody happy (which had in fact been her role in childhood); her absent father who had been separated from the home for many years, yet had remained curiously close to them; an uncle who had filled his place; her mother as the matriarchal head of the family; her psychopathic husband; his family clowning and whitewashing, which is what she had spent her life doing; clowning outwardly; making a court jester of herself, while secretly making a fool of someone else. . . .

Then she thought carefully about the dream and realized that the only element in the entire dream which was really clear (the rest being clouded in extrapolation), was the sense of her own hand in motion, of the whitewash or the white paint with which she painted the socket of the eye—the eye that was not there, the eye that could not see what she was up to. And then the eye she was painting out became the all-seeing Cyclopean eye of the analyst: and for the first time she began to think of her own future and of the freedom that lay ahead and of what she wanted and feared to do with it.

All of this poured from her in a rush. Suddenly one realized the fantastic condensation which had been achieved: a lifetime concentrate, distilled into the essence of one single multi-valent gesture, i.e., of whitewashing or painting out an eye in the eye-socket of the clown, analyst, patient, court jester: an expurging of the world within her and around her, out of her past and into her future. This single gesture covered many figures, many places, and many people. It was a binding of space and time. She dreamed with the same economy with which she painted. Yet the product of the dream was a purely idiosyncratic language which could carry meaning to no other human being, and not even to herself without the power of translation which she had acquired.

(6) A man returned from a long and difficult war to find that his wife had made up her mind to leave him. He knew that from her point of view she was right to do this. She was a gifted musician, chafing always at the dissipation of energy and attention which family life demanded, a bachelor-girl at heart, affectionate and gay but only when she could walk her own path. The children were grown, their own lives launched or launching. He knew that this was right for everyone and that he would get on all right, close to his children and friends and immersed in the work he cared about; but he was deeply saddened. He dreamed:

"They" were toiling up a rocky hill. Or rather they had climbed it; and as they stood at the top they surveyed a village nestling under the peak in a high mountain valley: small white houses, picket fences, a white church, all resembling the New England village of his childhood, glowing in the setting sun. "They," these undefined others, filed silently by him towards the little white houses and into the white church, as he stood in the lengthening shadows.

This man was an engineer: and the dream was his life's sad poem.

Of course all that he had actually dreamed was a single static scene, the high mountain village, plucked from the heartstrings of his childhood memories of New England, towards which his heart turned now in the sun and shadow of his afternoon. He had indeed led his brood up the rocky hill; and like Moses he watched them file by him. All the poignancy of his life was condensed into that one image out of a dream. Again one asks, can any art form do more?

(7) The extraordinary power of preconscious condensation is often demonstrated by a single thought, which reverberates through the mind like a haunting melody.

Thus, a young doctor returned from the fourth day of his training analysis. He was seated on the floor playing with his infant son; and as he played a sentence kept running through his mind. The sentence was "Tar-Baby ain't saying nothin'; and Brer Fox, he lay low." He had not thought of the Uncle Remus stories since his own childhood. In fact their roots went back to the death of his own mother in his third year, and to the Southern woman who had come to take care of him, and who had first read these stories to him. He was puzzled by the sudden re-emergence of this phrase at this time. Suddenly out of the past the entire Tar-Baby story came back to him, as fresh and vivid as though he had read it the day before. He remembered how Brer Rabbit came loping down the road, to find Tar-Baby sitting by the side of the road where Brer Fox had set him out as a trap for Brer Rabbit; how Brer Rabbit tried to strike up a friendly conversation, but how the Tar-Baby had not answered, so that Brer Rabbit became angry and hauled off and hit him first with one paw and then with the other, then with his hind feet, finally butting him with his head so that he was stuck to the Tar-Baby, at which Brer Fox rolled in the road laughing at him. In the end, however, Brer Rabbit had tricked Brer Fox into tearing him loose and throwing him into the briar patch. There he had run off and thumbed his nose at the fox, crying mockingly, "Bred and born in this briar patch, Brer Fox." Instantly it became clear to the young doctor that the haunting sentence from the beginning of the old folk-tale represented to him the entire dilemma in which he found himself at that very moment in his life. For four days he had been going to his analyst, trying to strike up a friendly conversation; and for four days, like Tar-Baby, his canny analyst had said nothing beyond a formal greeting and leave-taking. Yet he was stuck to his Tar-Baby, and to the analysis which offered the only solution to his bitterly painful domestic problems, while the foxy gods laughed. All of the young doctor's anger and frustration, all of his desire to be free of this silent Tar-Baby, plus all the echoes of his life reverberating through the years since his mother's death were condensed into this one sentence.

4. Examples from Finance

I will cite two examples of the role of preconscious processes in finance, and of the consequences which arise when their free function is distorted by unconscious processes.

(1) For emotional reasons a man whose IQ soared high had always been a mediocre student. His attention during his school and university years had been on many other activities. He was a last-minute-cram-boy who with the skill and speed of a final sprint would always pass with B's or upper C's. This was the only hint of the latent power that was released when events mobilized his full capacities.

His extraordinary preconscious ability first became manifest when a series of deaths placed him at the head of a large brokerage office, while he was still a young man. There he suddenly had to take full responsibility for split-second decisions, based on an instantaneous processing of many figures in his mind at the same time, including data which shifted constantly throughout each day. All of this was held in some fluid state in his thinking apparatus, not consciously yet effectively available; and on that basis he made his choices among immeasurable risks by feelings and intuitions. This measured his ability to be guided by preconscious perceptions of hundreds of factors affecting economic movements in the country as a whole. It soon became clear that this man was something of a genius. The deaths of which he was guiltless had eliminated all authoritarian figures from his life, releasing him to function fearlessly and guiltlessly on a preconscious level, to receive, record, utilize, integrate, and respond to the continuous bombardment from a preconscious assembly of data. He was known for the phenomenal accuracy with which his decisions predicted the future course of the market in several commodities and many stocks.

Then came several blows. Upon the sudden death of his mother, he developed potency difficulties with his wife. He began to flounder through a series of fruitless and unpleasant "affairs" in which he tried to reassure himself about his potency. At the same time a man he trusted betrayed him and shook the foundations of his whole financial empire. This started a desperate effort to recoup his losses, to prove himself both in bed and out of it. The self-doubts and anxieties which had made him a crybaby in childhood were relit. Ancient jealousies of two older brothers and of his father (all three of whom had died) took over completely. Under their dead but watchful and mocking eyes he became again a school-child, unable any longer to use his preconscious processes freely and creatively. Instead these became the enslaved servants of his conscious drive to retrieve his fortunes and to prove his potency, deformed by frantic, desperate, and conflicting needs which originated in areas of unconscious conflict, which derived from earliest childhood and which had been reactivated by his mother's death, the ensuing difficulties with his wife, and the betrayal by his friend. By destroying the family heritage he now destroyed his dead father's image. He became in fact a blind Samson, pulling down the pillars of the temple on himself, his wife, and the hated memory of his family. Having previously taken care of everyone, he was now executing a long-deferred vengeance: an unconscious patricidal and fratricidal Kentucky mountain feud against the older generation. These destructive impulses were infused also by deeply buried and unconscious problems of bitter latent homosexuality, and an even deeper need to change sides, to escape his imprisonment in manhood, to return to the crybaby, the "sissy," the little-girl image of his early years, when he had been happily tied to his mother. There was more to this: but these fragments are enough to illustrate the storm of destructive and financially irrelevant unconscious forces which had taken control of his preconscious processes deforming them to their own purposes, to the destruction of his creative life.

(2) I will give one other example of the distortion of preconscious function by unconscious processes in financial matters.

A man of considerable business and financial acumen and experience consulted a psychiatrist about one of his two sons. In due time the son was sent to a far city for treatment which ultimately turned out to be highly successful. It was only as it became clear that the treatment would succeed that the father came with considerable perplexity to recount the following story:

He explained that when the boys had been small, he had set up an account for each: and that he had traded for the two accounts equally and to the best of his knowledge and ability. For some years both accounts had gone equally well. Then he began to notice that a strange thing was happening: namely, that everything he did for one account turned out successfully, while everything he did for the other turned out to be unsuccessful. Here then was a man, using precisely the same intuitive, intellectual, and emotional machine, namely his own, and on identical problems: yet succeeding consistently with one account and consistently failing with the other. As he reviewed the situation more closely he was struck by the fact that everything always went well in the account that was for the benefit of the son about whom he had no anxieties and towards whom he felt an uncomplicated affection and pride. The other account was for the benefit of the son about whose health and future he was in a constant state of anguished uncertainty. Consciously he wanted above all else to make this lad at least financially secure. At the same time, however, he struggled with a mixture of resentment, anxiety, and hostility towards this lad, with whose difficulties he identified strongly yet unconsciously. It was here that the unconscious forces arose to play on his preconscious processes, leading him into such errors of judgment that on two occasions he had had to start the account over again.

77

5. Examples from Scientific Research

Scientific research offers endless examples of the ways in which forces which arise out of unconscious conflicts can warp and distort all free preconscious creativity.

(1) A drive for originality often is dismissed as originality for its own sake. Rarely is this true. Even the phrase, "for its own sake," actually begs the issue; because what appears in the form of a drive for originality usually cloaks many profound personality problems. A few obvious examples of these are a profound block over mastering facts, a fear of competition with others, limitless and insatiable megalomaniac ambitions, or an unconscious rejection of all existing authority.

(2) The conscious fears of exposing conclusions to public challenge may arise out of even more deeply buried unconscious terror of a more personal bodily exposure. These may combine in such a way as to compel an investigator to choose problems which will take a lifetime to solve. At times this is further concealed by fantasies of omnipotence and omniscience, masked under another layer of theoretical devotion to abstract or pure science (as in an artist the same unconscious fear of the bodily can masquerade as a pure devotion to the abstract in art). Thus layer upon layer of well-constructed rationalizations can disguise the true reason for a scientist's creative impotence, an impotence which is no measure of his latent creative capacities.

(3) Alternatively another anxiety-driven investigator may demand his reward every day; and may therefore be able to commit himself only to quick and easy research projects.

(4) Another pair of opposites is provided by two investigators, one of whom cannot rest until a pseudo-solution is in his hand: while his opposite number is afraid to find answers. Like a kleptomaniac the first may even be forced to falsify data in his desperate drive to achieve a feeling of knowing all the answers. The opposite is never so terrified as when he has found a likely answer. Therefore he postpones endlessly any ultimate coming to grips with a definitive test of his thesis. The one is unable to endure suspense or uncertainty for more than a few hours or days. The other is unable ever to allow himself to resolve his uncertainty, and is forced by his neurosis to remain suspended indefinitely in a state of obsessional doubt and indecision, rather than to resolve anything. (I have seen this well rationalized as the pure scientific spirit in an eminent, scholarly, but unproductive neuropathologist, and also in one of the truly great but most frustrated of psychiatrists.)

(5) There is the scientist who never can believe his own work, and has therefore to steal fragments from others. Data which have already proved his point always seem insufficient to him. In consequence he must add unnecessary data which he may even have had to make up. His parallel is the famous writer who had to hide in everything he wrote a few words and phrases lifted bodily from the writings of others.

(6) There is the scientist who pursues endless fathers, his life spent in progressing from one father to another, always starting a new career whenever he reaches the point of launching mature and independent work in the last.

(7) There is the anxiety-driven scientist who lives on a treadmill, who can never finish one piece of work without immediately being seized with terror that he never will be able to complete another. He can never lie fallow, never rest, never accept a moment's peace; because without work he is in a torment of anxiety. Without work he is not unlike the patient with a handwashing compulsion deprived of soap and water. And as he plunges headlong from one task to the next, he is brother to the artist who cannot let the paint dry on one canvas before he starts the next, for fear that he never will be able to paint again; or to the writer who is in the same predicament; or to the millionaire who can never stop accumulating.

These men do not break down from overwork. They suffer from a profound and complex compulsion which has taken over their normal creativity. "Success" always cheats them; because it never attains the unconscious goals of their activities. Indeed the successful among those who suffer from compulsive work drives actually break down into angry and anxious middle-year depressions more often than do those who fail in the same fields of work and who may have worked even harder. Therefore we can say with confidence that the breakdown is the result not of overwork but of insufficient insight. They break down into involutional depressions from the inevitable decompensation of compulsion neuroses which can never reach their goals.

These examples illustrate the fact that there are subtle elements in creative scientific research which are related to neurotic mechanisms. Furthermore in different successive phases, research demands different types of adjustment from its devotees. In the exploratory phase in which the scientist gathers data, he should make his observations free from preconceptions and preferential biases, and above all free from any drive to systematize the data prematurely. This requires a free, imaginative, flexible, uncommitted attitude in which preconscious functions can predominate. At a later phase more rigidly organized psychological processes are required to test and doubt and prove and doubt again, and then to rearrange and systematize the data. This demands a personality which can doubt on a consciously self-critical level, but without being trapped in obsessional indecision. It will have meticulous features which can readily merge with those of the obsessional-compulsion neurosis. Sometimes it moves closer to the tendency of the paranoid patient to organize his ideas into pseudological delusional systems. It has often been observed that as they fight about their theoretical conceptions, seemingly well-adjusted scientists may behave like paranoid patients. Were it not for their human right to anonymity, I could cite easily recognizable instances of this from the fields of mathematics, chemistry, biochemistry, biology, and endocrinology, from psychiatry and from psychoanalysis. These equal the bitter conflicts among schools of painting, of music, of literature, and the philosophy of aesthetics.

What all of this really goes to show is that the creative life in general makes extraordinary demands on the human personality. Specifically in science, creativity demands a flexibility which is perhaps greater than that of almost any other occupation to which man can dedicate himself. Precisely because the scientist must be as imaginative and free in fantasy as a poet, artist, or musician, and at the same time as tightly organized as the builder of bridges or the man who organizes and plans the split-second timing of an atomic explosion, we ask that the creative scientist should have a high degree of emotional and psychological freedom and imaginativeness coupled to an equal degree of organized precision. Few other occupations demand so much. I am not unhappy that science makes this demand of us. I am unhappy only at the fact that we do not recognize the implication of this demand and do nothing to help even the most gifted scientists attain the degree of emotional maturity and freedom which would make it possible for them to use their intellectual endowments in the most creative and constructive way that is possible for man to attain. I am unhappy at our complacency with a primitive educational process which to so large an extent re-enforces everything neurotic in human nature (cf. chapter III).

Let me illustrate this further in order to drive home its lesson.

In the papers published in the *American Scientist* (48), I gave several examples of scientific work which had been warped by the unconscious residue of repressed childhood pain and conflict.

(1) There was the man whose research in water-metabolism was biased by years of struggles with en uresis and the humiliations to which a hostile father had exposed him.

(2) There was the brilliant pharmacologist who became psychotic, but who in the years before his psychosis became evident did work in which the latent delusions influenced more and more his choice of the hypothesis about drugs and drug-action which he was trying to prove,

and finally the very techniques by which he tried to prove it.

(3) Another example was the inventor whose every invention in his earlier years had had only one goal: namely, to depreciate and ultimately to destroy his father.

(4) Still another was the scientist who was deeply and angrily defensive about his own mixed racial origins, and whose bitterness and anger invested every scientific controversy in which he became involved, even on matters having nothing to do with anthropology.

Balanced against these are those examples of scientific creativeness in which conscious and preconscious processes have held the upper hand over unconscious impediments, with the consequence that the creative process could function undistorted even in sleep.

(1) There is a brilliant example described by the American mathematician, L. E. Dixon (Hardamard, 23, page 7) of two sisters who were rivals in geometry. One of them had spent a long evening puzzling unsuccessfully over a problem and discussing it. The other dreamed the answer in her sleep, and talked in her sleep sufficiently clearly for the first sister to write it down. The following morning they were able to establish its accuracy.

(2) There is the well-known example given by Poincaré of how during a few minutes of abstracted preoccupation in a crowded bus the solution came to him for a problem in non-Euclidian geometry which had baffled him for months.

(3) There is the famous reverie by Kekulé of the snake swallowing its own tail, which illumined for him the structure of the benzene ring.

(4) There is the amusing example of the gynecologist who dreamed how to tie a surgical knot deep in the pelvis one-handed, and with his left hand at that. Here one can recognize the imprint of concurrent conscious, preconscious, and unconscious determinants with transparent clarity.

(5) There is Otto Loewe's account of the derivation of the whole neurohumoral concept from a dream.

There are many comparable examples from the arts, music, poetry (A. E. Housman, Lamartine, Mozart, etc.) (19).

Certainly such experiences justify the conviction that the processes of free association, which shake us out of our ruts, thereby make it possible to bring together new combinations of ideas, allowing these new combinations to fall into recognizable patterns without the participation of full consciousness. In fact, new syntheses fall into place precisely when we do not imprison them in that limiting process which we call conscious thinking, and when preconscious syntheses form without interference from unconscious determinants.

In my own work I have found this to be true so frequently that I deliberately plan my work in that way. I will regularly work on a problem late into the evening and until I am tired. The moment my head touches the pillow I fall asleep with the problem unsolved. Frequently I will awaken four or five hours later, sometimes in the middle of the very sentence on which I was hung up as I went to sleep, but with a new assembly of the material. This will almost surely be forgotten unless I dictate or write a note about it at once.

The same process may sometimes occur when I am driving a car, or riding, or while listening to music.

One theoretical suggestion which I look upon as the most hopeful clue which I have ever pursued towards an understanding of the essential differences between the neurotic and the psychotic processes arose out of a moment in which, on subsequent reflection, I could trace the concurrent influence of several unconscious and preconscious symbolic processes. The clue in question has to do with what I subsequently called the bipolar anchorage of the symbolic process, meaning by this that every symbol must have roots simultaneously in the internal perceptual experiences of the body and in the external perceptual experiences of the outer world. The moment of birth of this hypothesis had a particular relationship to the well-worn path between my office and the Medical Center, one end representing the internal and the other the external world. This was a preconscious allegorical pattern which had deeper roots as well, roots in problems which at one period in my own development reflected unconscious conflicts over sexual identification and sibling rivalry. These early conflicting identifications with an older sister and an older brother (a powerful and naturally gifted athlete) paralleled, infused, and also confused the issue of whether to go into psychiatry or into experimental neuropathology. Psychological vs. organic had meant to me both woman versus man and internal versus external.

With all of these alternatives deep in the background, I drove home from the hospital late one night in a somnolent state. My whole body and the car and the route of my drive became a hazy, symbolic representation of these conflicts. In an almost dreamlike fashion these deep levels of personality organization were translated onto another level, i.e., that of scientific issues; and out of these precipitated an hypothesis concerning symbolic functions. The route between office and hospital became both the symbolic bridge between neurosis and psychosis, and at the same time the bridge between tensions generated on the psychological level of experience and its translation into somatic dysfunction. The bipolar route between office and hospital became the bipolar symbol, which in turn suggested by extrapolation that this bipolarity of all symbolic processes might be at least one of the links for which we have long been seeking, which would make understandable the translation of psychological experience into somatic disturbances and vice versa.

In science such a moment of apparent illumination is never an ultimate act of faith, as it might be for the theologian or for the poet and artist. It is rather the starting point for an investigation; but it supplies the investigator both with a beckoning goal and a *vis-a-tergo* without which nothing new is ever discovered. Yet if the ancient personal conflicts to which I have referred had still been deeply buried and overladen with distorting disguises instead of standing clearly in the light of preconscious understanding, their contribution to the final conceptual product would have been to distort it rather than to help in the production of a potentially useful scientific allegory.

6. Examples from Literature and the Plastic Arts

(1) A writer who had had two successes became totally blocked. He could complete nothing that he at-

tempted. Indeed he was so blocked that, as he told me subsequently, his ulcers were activated and he had to be hospitalized. Suddenly while in the hospital his imagination was caught by a theme which wrote itself. The writing went so smoothly that it was like a release from his personal prison; and he could not bring himself to stop long enough to examine it critically. He did not recognize even the possibility that its compelling quality might have no greater aesthetic value than any other neurotic compulsion. Instead he attributed to it an origin in some higher imperative. Therefore as he poured his heart out in his writing, he produced a novel which except for one beautiful bit of characterization and one superb scene was a distillate of unconscious contempt and hatred toward his wife, his friends, and associates, and especially towards everyone who had helped and supported and carried him through difficult years. The accumulation of a lifetime of hatred was poured out in transparent mockery of all who had befriended him. Of this he was blandly unaware. He had a feeling that because the novel wrote itself with such unchecked violence, this betrayal of human values carried its own justification.

(2) Another writer, a man of great experience and depth of insight, came to realize that in the communication of ideas he operated not as one person but two. When *talking* he expressed all the love and affection and warmth towards humanity of which he was capable. When *writing*, on the other hand, he was shooting from a concrete pillbox, and out came all his bitterness and hatred. On one occasion the result of this was that a tale, the planning of which had arisen out of a full heart and with humanity of spirit, became infected as he wrote it

with a niggling bitterness and anger, so that it became destructive and hostile. His unconscious hate took over, took the writing out of his hands, shaping it to its own ends. The result was a piece of work which had been planned with compassion, as an apostrophe to all the greater strivings of human nature pitted against human triviality, but which had become nothing but a gesture of contempt towards the friends and associates he pilloried. A social tragicomedy became a travesty and a burlesque.

(3) De Voto describes this clearly in one of his studies of Mark Twain (11).

(4) I could cite artists and writers who inflate trivial ideas into something of vast pseudo-importance: and could set them over against others who start with a magnificent canvas, and then under the influence of their inner terrors end up with whimsical miniatures (Blackmur, 4).

(5) Or one may see the play of unconscious forces in the determination of aesthetic values. For instance, a brilliantly gifted painter had worked out a complete system of aesthetics, by which she could prove that cities are places of great beauty, and the country a place of great ugliness. She claimed that it was because "cities are beautiful" and because "aesthetic values must never be denied" that she chose to live in the city. This was a brilliant tour-de-force; but it masked the fact that she had a terror of sunlight and shadow, of the rustling of wind in bushes and trees or through the grasses. Therefore in the country she was beset with terror; and more patently than is usually the case her entire pseudo-aesthetic construct was a brilliant rationalization of her personal escape from fear.

(6) Early in childhood a youngster had overheard a doctor telling his parents that he had severe congenital heart lesions, possibly complicated by acute rheumatic fever with an endocarditis, that he did not have long to live, that he would not be able to take part in any physical activity, that he would have to lead the life of a cardiac invalid. All of this proved to be erroneous; but it was several years before the mistake was detected and verified, the diagnosis corrected, and the bans lifted. In the meantime he had entrenched himself in invalidism, and had devoted himself to a lethargic kind of painting, and this in spite of the fact that his inherent gifts were of a high order. Indeed even after the correction had been made, he found it almost impossible to accept the correction, and often used the illusion of cardiac disease as an excuse to avoid all challenge of vigorous competition with other youngsters, and subsequently the challenge of sex. Inwardly he was corroded with envy, jealousy, and hatred. Outwardly he was evasive, obsequious, and ingratiating. The inner hate expressed itself in everything he painted: in the content of his work, the colors that he chose, the harshness of his treatment of the material. Painting became the vehicle for his deeply buried hate and envy. Any contact with a man whom he looked upon as physically better endowed than himself, or any contact with a woman to whom he felt attracted aroused a shaking storm of hatred. Yet of this he was totally unaware. All that he knew was the compulsive frenzy to turn to his "art" which seized him at such moments. Nor was his art devoid of success. Quite on the contrary, he won world-wide fame and recognition. This however brought no ease to his spirit; and as the years went on, his productivity was

hampered until in the course of time he was no longer able to free his preconscious even to a limited degree except by saturating himself with drugs and alcohol. Meanwhile unconscious rage continued to distort the products of his great talent to an ever more grotesque degree.

One could hardly find a better laboratory demonstration of what a rampant unconscious need for vengeance and destruction can do to even the most gifted creative preconscious powers.

(7) The lawyer-poet, Melville Cane, in a brief but penetrating volume entitled Making a Poem (9), has described simply, directly, and unpretentiously the precision and the beauty of the preconscious heart of the creative process. It contains a few parenthetical references to technical analytical literature. In these for a brief instant he obscures the simple directness of the self-observations, which give his book its unique value as source material. Yet even Melville Cane slips into the old, established, and mistaken concept. Thus on page 11 he writes that "the unconscious is the reservoir of the material from which one draws." Later on the same page he describes the process with great simplicity and precision, but repeats the error: "I don't try to think and I don't try not to think: I do, however, try to make myself comfortable and free from bodily strains. After a while I become gradually relaxed—the deeper the passivity, the closer one draws to the unconscious." My insistence on the substitution of the concept of Preconscious is more than a mere semantic clarification.

I mention this not in criticism but merely to indicate how completely the misuse of the concept of the unconscious has permeated all thinking and writing in this area. Substitute "preconscious" and the argument is back on the right track, and undercuts the whole structure of misunderstandings, as a consequence of which his neurosis has come to be the most prized possession of the creative person, as though his life as a creator depended on the untouchability of the neurotic process itself.

(8) Another erudite, urbane, profound, wise, and thoughtful book (Hitschmann, 25) contains a rich mine of data with which to supplement the approach to the problem under discussion. Furthermore, together with the foreword by Ernest Jones and the editorial preface by Sydney Margolin, it contains additional leads into the literature. Dr. Hitschmann's own introduction gives us a swift survey of the first tentative and exciting explorations into the psychoanalytic studies of writers, religious leaders, and philosophers with which the early psychoanalysts were preoccupied in the first two decades of the century, an interest recently rekindled by Greenacre (21), Oberndorf (67), and others. Implicit here is the story of a cultural revolution which has evolved in part with the spread of psychoanalytic understanding throughout our entire culture. Inevitably any such period of rapid sociocultural change is attended by some degree of confusion, confusions arising from changes in the psychoanalytic theory and from its misapplications, and confusions resulting from the resistance to change which is deeprooted in all human nature and most particularly in the creative man. It is my hope that this approach to the problem may reopen it to an objective and critical reevaluation. Above all, as will be indicated in the final chapter, I hope that it will challenge the complacency

of those educational conventions which, it is my contention, tend to paralyze and block rather than to free and facilitate that great creative potential which is far more widespread in human nature than is generally acknowledged. In *Great Men* (25) Dr. Hitschmann describes some of those exceptions whose creative potential somehow survived, however warped and distorted and battered by their own neuroses and by the "educational" processes to which they were subjected. I think it is fair to say that humanity can do better than this if it puts its mind to it (51, 53).

Ghiselin (19) has assembled relevant data from noted mathematicians, musicians, philosophers, painters, writers, sculptors, dancers, psychologists, and physiologists, covering a span of many years.

Everyone finds what he is looking for when he turns to material such as this. Certainly it seems to me that I can find in the self-descriptions of these many diverse creative folk, sometimes with a slight rephrasing or alteration of emphasis, ample justification for the thesis which I am defending. Whether others will find in these same communications a validation of my thesis or its correction, or even its confutation, remains to be seen. I will not attempt to misuse the material by picking phrases out of context here and there just to give a spurious backing to my own theory. I will say only that personally I find much corroboration in these pages. I respect the possibility that in this I may delude myself; but I hope that if others will approach it with an effort to divest themselves of prior conceptions, they may also find support for the thesis which I present. I believe that I harbor this hope not merely because it is mine; but also because it seems to me to show us a way out of what is otherwise an insoluble dilemma.

7. Distortions in Art and Science

It is hard to characterize the subtle similarities and differences between those processes which create by searching out and integrating the flexible multivalences of preconscious symbolic functions and those which end in illness or in the corruption of the creative process itself through the distortions imposed by unconscious symbolic functions. Yet these are what make the differences between the spontaneous and nearly automatic mathematical creativity of Poincaré, and that of the brilliant, young mathematical physicist who had an orgasm on completing an original solution of a problem for which he was not trained and then went into a panic and disappeared for a week in a state of catatonic confusion and mingled excitement and depression.

This obscurity is due in part to the fact that we still lack instruments by which to estimate, even approximately, the relative roles of the three conceptual and symbolic systems which participate concurrently in all such phenomena, i.e., in the imaginative creations of health and in the equally imaginative creations of illness. The development of such an instrument is one of the urgently needed additions to the techniques of psychological exploration and therapy. Without such instruments the best we can do is to indicate, as I have tried to do, some of the more obvious ways in which these distorting forces operate. As a further result of these limitations, comparisons of the roles of the three symbolic systems in art and science must be limited to a few cautious hints.

In their vulnerability to different kinds of distorting influences pure research and abstract art have certain features in common. This is true also of applied research and representational art. One might say that in this respect basic science is to applied science as abstract art is to representational art. All four start from the familiar. Applied science and the more literal forms of art and literature reproduce these with as little alteration, distortion, or fragmentation as possible. In this process, projection plays a relatively secondary role although it is not excluded. Pure research and the more abstract forms of art and literature on the contrary dissect the units of experience, rearrange the pieces, juggle them around, and juxtapose them out of context. The outcome of this process cannot fail to bear the imprint of multiple projections of buried and often predominantly unconscious aspects of the personality of the abstract artist, or of the basic scientist.

As a consequence the dominant sources of distortion differ in these two pairs of creative processes. In applied research external pressures predominate among the sources of distortion. These are manifested in the influence of pursuit of money, status, and fame, in the immediate alleviation of anxiety, in the urgent demand to satisfy immediate practical, commercial, military, or humanistic purposes, etc. For example, in the entire field of applied scientific research I know of no external source of distortion greater than is the eagerness of the physician to find a cure, an eagerness which derives simultaneously from social pressures, from humanitarian impulses, and from more deeply egocentric needs. (Freud commented long since on the unconscious sadistic purposes which may at times masquerade in this disguise.)

In pure research, on the other hand (as in abstract art), the major sources of distortion are internal; and the products of the creative processes bear to a more unique degree the imprint of buried and unresolved neurotic problems. This can be in the same moment highly creative and so idiosyncratic as to be as uncommunicable as are the neologisms of a schizophrenic.

These differences in the vulnerability of the two types of scientific research are closely paralleled by differences in the vulnerability of the two types of creative art and literature. It would not be possible however or even profitable to pursue this line of reasoning further at this time.

We might in fact range the upper reaches of creative activity in a continuous spectrum, at one end of which would be all the precise factual, objective, representational forms of human endeavor, i.e., all efforts to reproduce facsimiles of the outside world and of the forces which are at work in that world, and to communicate clearly about them. At the next band would be our efforts to express and communicate the feelings which are aroused by the interaction between these external events and our internal conflicts. At the far end of the spectrum would be all efforts to communicate and yet at the same time to hide these very conflicts. Applied science lies at the first pole; and with many intergrades, pure science lies at the second. Similarly, literal and representative art is close to the first; abstract art, to the second. Yet there are unconscious projections of buried conflicts in even the most practical fruits of the labors of the utilitarian scientist or representational artist; just as there are residual imprints of the real world in the dreamlike speculations of the most abstract scientific worker or in the output of the most impressionistic artist. Thus all such pairs of polar opposites represent extreme bands on a nearly continuous spectrum.

Here, as in so many things having to do with the neurotic process, we tend to be influenced too greatly by secondary differences. All of the external features of the life which the creative man leads must vary with the form which his creativity assumes. There is a wide difference in the quality and flavor of the life of an artist as contrasted with that of the scientist. There are differences in the way they use day and night, in the meanings to them of work and play, in the immediate and derivative expressions of their instinctual drives, in their use of language symbols and of plastic hieroglyphics. All such secondary differences have misled us into assuming that the creative process itself must be basically different in the two. Yet there is actually no evidence that creativity in the scientist differs from creativity in the artist more widely than the differences which occur regularly among different kinds of scientific work. Under analysis, one finds that in spite of secondary variations the creative process has far more in common across the broad tapestry of human creative activities than is usually assumed.

A few last illustrations will, I hope, give substance to this general statement.

A soft-voiced taxi-driver said to his fare, "It always moves me so to watch a seeing-eye dog at work." He perceived and felt and spoke as a poet, and his words had qualities of reality, of a dream, of a song, and of a poem. Many meanings were latent in his simple words: e.g., the nostalgia of the adult for childhood and mother, and the consequent pervasive mythology of adult helplessness; the residue in adult years of the child's fantasy of a world in which children take over; the adult's fantasy of a world in which the wisdom of the child is all the wisdom that adult life requires (i.e., the essence of the Christ-Child myth, as embodied in the old phrase, "And a little child shall lead them"); the expansion of this myth to include the fantasy of being led and cared for by an animal, a variant of which is the Mowgli fable in its many forms. All of this rich lore is hidden in the sensitive and poetic response of the taxi driver to a simple scene.

It is at the same time a peculiarly apt example of how the synthetic element in the creative process takes as its point of departure the day's emotionally unfinished business and projects this onto the external stimuli of human events, precisely as we do in dreams or in a Rorschach test, or in a Thematic Apperceptive device, or in vivid hypnagogic reveries; yet drawing at the same time from deeper unconscious material.

Meanwhile, this complex pattern is enriched ceaselessly by preconscious processes of photographic and phonographic impressions. These are recorded wordlessly and automatically. If then this achieves no conscious re-representation, if the entire process is allowed to reach final expression as a product of preconscious and unconscious processes alone, there can be little selectivity and no critique.

On the expressive side of the creative process, whether we deal with unskilled labor or the simple skills of an artisan, or the highest forms of artistic, literary, and scientific virtuosity, variations in skill and craftsmanship are also woven into the pattern of creativity.

Yet locked in battle with the need to show and to communicate is the need to hide: and every man both shows and hides himself in his every action. A five-year-old runs naked and gleaming in the sun, shouting, "I can't go in swimming without my bathing suit. It isn't customary." Every activity is thus a self-stripping and a masquerade behind which the *I-Me-Myself* of the doer can hide. Doctors, teachers, lawyers, professors, painters, writers, scientists, and workmen: all may express and hide themselves in the same productive act.

This source of distortion can take many forms. There is the poetess who can write the beginnings and the ends of every sentence *but never the middle*,[1] and who similarly has always to hide the middle of her body even in her love-making, so as to maintain her sexual ambiguity. There is the renowned educator for whom the written word is an act of decorum, the spoken word an act of defiant public auto-erotism, in the very face of his father. There is the experienced public speaker for whom writing was the distillation of hate, and the lecture platform an appeal for love so intense that it always made him feel genitally exposed. There was a gifted young economist

---

[1] This statement could be amplified to include not only the middles of long sentences as opposed to their beginnings and ends but also the same components of paragraphs and stories. Around the edges she felt relaxed and safe. At the heart of things she became tense and tight and would literally bog down and not be able to move. She would start sentences and become blocked at the halfway point. To observe what happened, I had her write free associative material in my presence; I also had her talk aloud as she wrote, so that I could tell exactly where she bogged down. Though the material itself would be more convincing than my description, considerations of privacy, apart from technical difficulties, make precise quotations impossible. Incidentally, I have seen a similar thing happen in relation to painting and sculpture.

who had to leave every sentence incomplete, all subjects and verbs but no objects, and sometimes just subjects alone without verb or object. Contrariwise there is the writer for whom every sentence, paragraph, and article had to be Minerva emerging fully formed and fully armed from the head of Zeus, and who therefore was often stalled before he started, because he could not always be sure that he was about to produce Minerva in one great cranial birth-pang.

Moreover in any one person different forms of communication are used to communicate and to hide different facets of the personality. In part the obscurities of modern art, literature, and music grow out of man's reticence about making a public show of his private neurosis except to a select inner circle; and this reticence wars with the defiant impulse of Everyman (and Woman) to be Gypsy Rose Lee.

I could describe one writer for whom the spoken word is always an instrument of hate and the written word an appeal for love. I could cite two others for whom precisely the opposite is true. I could cite a great musician for whom music performed is an act of hate, and music composed is an act of love; and another for whom precisely the opposite is true.

As a further complication we must recognize that the act of communication is overburdened with conflicting meanings, whether we communicate by word or color, or line drawn or shape or sound. Each of these is always in some hidden and varying measure an instrument of magic: a magic for changing one's self or the world around one, a magic for doing and undoing, for achieving and denying, for exhibiting and hiding, for smashing and

99

for integrating, for killing and for succoring. All of this is true whether the instrument for communication is being used in analysis or in literature and poetry, in studies of economics, government, or history, in prayer, in the fairy tales, songs, and lullabies of childhood, or in the fulmination of the liberal or the fascist. In considering these paradoxes it is fatal to overlook such obvious facts as that all of the instruments of man's highest creativity are used as substitutes for action. At most they are to move others to act, not the creator. So that over the very phenomena of creativity we face an eternal war between the wordless man of action and the actless man of words: a warfare that colors our culture and that operates within every creative man.

Let me bring this to a close with two final examples.

A writer went through an intricate and profoundly revealing day of torment. He brought with him to his analytic hour an advance copy of his newest book. He himself described his need to give an inscribed copy to the analyst as "strongly compulsive." It was an advance copy; and he battled with the fear of what this might reveal about the analytic relationship if someone else should open the volume and see the inscription, no matter how formal and noncommittal were his words. Would the analyst carelessly allow it to lie around? Would the analyst *not* be there when he arrived, with the result that the writer would have to carry it away with him, so that he would then be burdened with this incriminating evidence for all the rest of that day? Would he make a mistake and switch two books, giving the analyst the copy inscribed to someone else, and the one inscribed to the analyst to a skeptical, anti-analytic friend, thus bringing hoots of derision down on his own head?

Under the impact of these torturing doubts he began to despise the volume itself as an expression of a need to curry favor. Then by opposites the book became something "filthy" which he had thrown out of his body, and which he was ready to present to the analyst no longer as a love-token but as a gesture of scorn. Then his secret, angry contempt for all writing came out, and especially for his own: "To Hell with it all—let us do nothing about it. Why did I ever write it? Why ever write at all? Only action counts." The whole body is a degraded, debased, animated, mobile, dirt-factory—everything in the body a decomposition product, a product of rotting and of death; every body-product a step towards death: saliva, tears, nasal drippings, urine, sweat, feces, blood, hair, semen, vaginal secretion—everything—*even breath and words themselves* became the decomposition products of the death process. Analysis itself was a dirty game—two people swapping the decomposing humors of the human spirit. No wonder he had to hide it. How, he asked, at length had he ever been able to write at all? I must add that this was a creative writer of extraordinary gifts and of world-wide recognition, translated into many tongues. Yet nothing could more clearly demonstrate the fantastic, subtle interweaving of the sick and the well, of the greatness of creativity and the destructiveness of the unconscious. And all of this was condensed into one single issue: should he give the analyst an inscribed copy of his book, or not?

In a quieter vein, I think of the dream of a physician as he approached the end of his analysis, with moving changes in his personality and profound depths of insight. He was a man who had once rather fancied that he looked like Sir Anthony Eden. All that he dreamed was that he was attending an international conference or congress. At least this was all that he recalled of the dream at first: congress or conference, science or politics, an old dilemma condensed into the one word, with implicit connotations which involved his relationship to his father, who had been a diplomat and who had wanted his son to follow in his footsteps. Then he thought of Eden and of what Eden meant to him: a man who took his father's (father-in-law's, i.e., Churchill's) place; of Eden's divorce and the patient's own terror lest analysis would lead him to divorce, and divorce to the Garden of Eden, where like Adam he would be tempted. This suddenly brought back to his mind one repressed image from the dream: to wit, that in the dream he had introduced Eden to his unmarried sister. The patient had brought into the analysis powerful but unconscious incestuous drives towards this sister. These had long since become conscious and attenuated. They were reactivated momentarily as he approached the end of treatment. Eden thus became his protection against this old incestuous drive; yet at the same time, since he and Eden were one, Eden became also the snake in the Garden of Eden through whom vicariously he could live out his incest. Yet out of this intricate network of thought and feeling, all that the patient dreamed was two brief flashes: an international conference or congress, and introducing Eden to his unmarried sister. These flashes were coded signs which represented the entire drama of his life, binding time and space, the near and the far, the past and the future into one "blip." This is creativity and the neurotic process at work.

For none of us would this be possible were it not for the continuous and spontaneous flow of associative material, on all three levels simultaneously: i.e., on *conscious* levels, where the current of fantasy is slow, intermittent, limited, and verbally sharply differentiated and precise; on *preconscious* levels of allegory, where the current is turbulent, free, and swift, tossing up all manner of strange and unexpected shapes out of the churning depths; on *unconscious* levels, where again the current is slower, stylized, rigid, condensed, stereotyped, unmoving, uncreative, and underground. It is out of the parallel flow of these three streams and their incessant interweaving that the creative processes and the processes of illness evolve.

Chapter 3

Education for Preconscious Freedom and its Relation to Creativity and to the Process of Maturation

1. INTRODUCTION

I must introduce this chapter by saying that it may be heavy going and possibly bad-tempered. This is because I am impatient with educators and psychiatrists, with scientists and artists, with all of us in fact, and always for the same thing: namely, for our complacency, for our failure to demand higher goals, and for the ineptitude with which we fail to turn criticism of education into the experimental search for new ways.

My central thesis will be that we do not need to be taught to *think*: indeed that this is something that cannot be taught. Thinking processes actually are automatic, swift, and spontaneous when allowed to proceed undisturbed by other influences. Therefore, what we need is to be educated in how not to interfere with the inherent capacity of the human mind to think. We need also to be helped to acquire the tools of communication: i.e., how to read and listen to words, how to speak and write them.

[1] This lecture borrows and extends the material presented in two previous lectures, both of which have been printed as transactions of the respective conferences: (1) On October 18, 1956, at the dedication of the Basic Sciences Building of the Downstate Medical Center of the State University of New York in Brooklyn. This was a conference on Pre-professional Education for Medicine. (2) On February 2, 1957, at the celebration of the Fortieth Anniversary of the Bank Street College of Education in New York City, on Problems of Depth and Scope in Education. In this conference my own contribution was on Education and Maturity.

Yet even this is only one component in the complex art of communication: since here again the more imperative need is to learn how not to let unconscious needs and conflicts and affects and defenses distort the work of the fully educated eye and ear and tongue and hand, lest these unconscious forces alter what we perceive in the act of apperceiving, and alter in the very act of communicating that which we have set out to communicate.

My point is that education will continue to perpetrate a fraud on culture until it accepts the full implications of the fact that the free creative velocity of our thinking apparatus is continually being braked and driven off course by the play of unconscious forces. Educational procedures which fail to recognize this end up by increasing the interference from latent and unrecognized neurotic forces.

Let me give a few random examples of the failure of education, as we know it, to deal adequately with this intricate problem. Each of these examples will be drawn from youngsters of superior endowments and achievements. Examples of more diffuse distortion and blocking will come later. Some are drawn from a previous publication (42).

(1) A brilliant lad in mid-adolescence, always an eager student, always priding himself on getting his work in on time, finds himself unable even to start, much less to complete, a theme on the history of the Oedipus myth. Instead, he becomes quite uncharacteristically depressed and surly and irritable with every fresh start. Finally the paralysis begins to invade other areas of work. Even his unusually imaginative and friendly teacher is unable to help. Nor does this teacher seem to realize how atypical

of the student's usual relaxed adjustment is his behavior at this time. An older relative, used "to listening with the third ear," finally persuades the boy to tell him the basic Oedipal tale. He notes that the lad tells it flawlessly, except that (as happens so often in recounting a dream) he omits two critical points: to wit, that the king that Oedipus murders was his father, and that the queen he marries was his mother. Can any educational system educate when teachers are too naïve to realize the dynamic significance of such myths in human life, and therefore too naïve to be alert to the unconscious meanings of this youngster's blocked state?

(2) Consider also the interplay of forces which surrounded first the imprisonment and then the release of another child, as he made his transition from day school to boarding school. This devoted youngster of thirteen had always been "a good boy" and a good student, a good little citizen in a conventional but thoughtful day school. For many reasons having to do with the complex nature of his relationship to his home, when he went to boarding school he felt lost, bewildered, frightened, and confused, both in class and out. He dropped swiftly from the top to the bottom of his class. In that same unhappy year he took leave of childhood in another sense by growing ten inches to become the tallest in his class. His voice changed. He became hairy. He was the only boy who had to shave daily. He felt "like a stupid lout." He had his first wet-dreams and his first struggles with masturbation.

His father, noting what had happened, wanted to build a bridge for him from school to home. He thought imaginatively in terms of a symbol of transportation, which led him to do something which would be frowned upon by most pedagogues. As the boy and his father wandered around the Auto Show together admiring a "sports" model, he offered the boy the car if he could climb back to somewhere near the top of the class where he belonged.

I shall not try to enter into or describe the underlying problems, but shall limit myself to pointing out that the gift relieved the lad of his paralyzing sense of guilt and loss. Without effort the boy could again read and listen and understand and recall. Within two months he had made an effortless leap to the top three in a large class in one of our most difficult preparatory schools.

This was, of course, a fortunate stroke in the dark. It left many things unresolved. I describe this not as an example to be followed universally, but to illustrate certain other points. Through his unusually sensitive, intuitive rapport with his son, this father was able to make a gesture which unlocked the boy's spontaneous use of his own latent abilities. In this particular situation, had the school handled the problem with punitive or disciplinary techniques it would have driven the boy deeper into guilt and depression, with consequences which might have paralyzed him in his subsequent academic career both in school and college. This is an example of the importance of developing techniques by which we can explore such situations fully enough to be able to tell when to depend upon the distribution of rewards and punishments and even sometimes a symbolic bribe. The argument is certainly not to be taken as a universal defense of bribery, punishment, or rewards, but as an example of the need for flexibility and precision. However, this will flow from a deeper knowledge of what is going on than is available to us under ordinary educational circumstances. Any effort to implement the theoretical solution encounters many practical problems of personnel and training. This, however, is another story.

(3) A brilliant young girl in early adolescence developed a passionate interest in Greek sculpture, costumes, culture, political organization, and literature. Then suddenly her interest evaporated. She stopped all studying, and from being a leader in her class dropped to the bottom. On investigation it gradually came to light that what had captured this youngster's interest in Greek civilization was the fact that the men and women seemed to dress alike. This meant to her that they were alike; that this had been a world in which the difference between herself and her brother, a difference against which she was rebelling, did not exist. A chance remark from her teacher about the homosexual implications of this culture had exploded this fantasy, and had plunged the girl into a depression in which she felt enraged, cheated, and resentful. It was this disillusionment which had initiated her unwitting sit-down strike.

(4) A little boy of seven became in essence a cartographer. Not only did he take great joy in the most painstaking and meticulous execution of maps, but he also memorized time-tables of train services all over the world. He became the class spokesman in all matters that had to do with things geographical. Geography led to history, history to politics, politics to the law. There, unfortunately, he tumbled into an illness which had many serious schizophrenic features. It was not an irreversible illness, however; and in the course of time and as the result of long searching treatment, the meaning of his early in-

terests came to light. He had lost his mother in a foreign land when he was four. Then shortly before he was seven he was taken on a trip, and during his absence his nurse died on a visit to her home in Scotland. In each instance death had been described to him as "going away"; and the youngster's heart was caught up in an unconscious fantasy of finding again the two women whom he had loved and lost. (I have seen the same kind of response more than once as a reaction to the early death of a parent who was far away at the time.)

(5) Another lad at an early age became a radio expert in a modern school. He built many radios, but he never played them. An obsessive preoccupation with electricity carried him through school and college and into graduate training in mathematical and nuclear physics. Then came a catastrophic breakdown when he found that mathematical thinking was touching off violent erotic excitement, often culminating in orgasm. Illness brought him to treatment. Treatment led back to earlier sources of his illness, *which were identical with the original roots of his interest in radio*. This had started with a panic at the sound of a telephone bell, a panic which in turn was related to many highly charged early problems, the nature of which I need not discuss here, beyond saying that the radio meant keeping in touch with his absent father to protect himself against certain fears which were generated by his mother's overstimulation of erotic fantasies and needs.

(6) Let me give one other illustration. A gay, eager, and extremely intelligent youngster, always the leader in her class, went through a long series of special interests: American Indians, Vikings, writing, painting, the modern

dance, piano, economics, and several others. This had begun with Indians and Vikings. She wrote stories about Indian and Viking boys. She painted their pictures. She dressed up to look like them. She acted their roles in the little plays which she wrote. Later she danced them. It turned out that in all of these "interests" she was acting out in varied forms her fantasies of being made over in her older brother's image. In the end, however, since every activity left her unaltered, and since everything that she attempted failed to work the magical change which she was seeking, she ran through such a long series of inconstant interests and in spite of exceptional endowments ended up stalled and inert and indifferent.

2. Culture and Education
The Indices of Failure

It has long been known that in early years children have an extraordinarily inventive imagination, transposing experience freely among the various sensory modalities, using delightful and original figures of speech and allegory. Thus a little boy of five had a drawing and a name for each day in the week. One was "stars and marrow," another was "black slide," a third was a "red stove," etc. This is the natural mode of the symbolic language of childhood; and, as I pointed out in an earlier article (30), it is rooted equally in the internal experiences of the body and the concurrent experiences of external percepts. Another little boy is a poet as he sits on his potty and passes wind and then says, "There's the whistle; now the train will come along." What happens to this poetic gift under the stultifying impact of that which we call our educational system? Lois Murphy has amassed evidence of this culturally imposed sterilization of the spontaneous creativity of childhood in her studies of the art of childhood (62; see also Loewenfeld, 62A).

Let me rephrase this ancient problem by asking what happens to the free play of preconscious functions in the course of conventional education?

My unhappy conviction is that much of the learning which has traditionally been looked upon as an essential attribute of the educated man has no necessary relevance either to creativity or to maturity, and that instead many ingredients in the process by which men become learned tend actively to obstruct them both. It seems that it is not learning or the learning process which matures men; it is maturity, however won, which makes it possible for learning to become creative.

I must warn that I am not going to suggest remedies for this state of affairs, nor detail any preventive measures. I will limit myself to an attempt to point out that there is in fact a state of illness in the educational body. The physician is so accustomed to being in this position that he is surprised when it arouses popular indignation. The doctor knows that for many years he may be able only to recognize that something is wrong, slowly adding to this the ability to define its nature. These two steps constitute the process of diagnosis; and he takes it for granted that they may precede even by generations the moment when increasing knowledge will enable him to contribute to prevention or therapy. In the history of medical science there have been only a few exceptional instances in which successful treatment or prevention has preceded diagnosis.

Social phenomena are even more complex than physiological ills, since in social problems physiological, economic, social, psychological, and developmental variables are concurrently operative. Nevertheless, people become unjustifiably angry if anyone points out that something is wrong in politics, economics, social organization, the family, or education, unless the prophet of doom simultaneously offers a remedy. It is to forestall this misplaced indignation that I emphasize at the outset that I will offer no easy solutions to the problems I will describe. Since educators and people generally must first acknowledge that something is amiss before they will begin the search for remedies, I will be content if I am able to convince even a few that there is something quite basically wrong with our approach to education, and if I can define what is wrong in terms of the crippling influence on the creative process of much of what occurs in school. Only at the end will I suggest a few directions in which it is reasonable to seek for corrective or preventive techniques. This is as far as I will presume to go; but I hope that experienced educators, with their more intimate knowledge of the details of educational procedures, may be able to offer more definitive remedies. Indeed, some educators and certain special schools have long since begun to attack the problems described. But I must leave this to them. My function is to challenge, not to offer panaceas.

The premises from which I start are not happy ones. Yet they are not pessimistic either, since they carry the implication that if we face these problems fearlessly we can solve them, and that if we solve them we will open a new era in human culture. Let me then state these premises:

(1) The great cultural processes of human society, including art and literature, science, education in general, the humanities and religion, have three essential missions—namely: to enable human nature itself to change; to enable each generation to transmit to the next whatever wisdom it has gained about living; to free the enormous untapped creative potential which is latent in varying degrees in the preconscious processes of everyone. It is my belief that in all three respects all of our great cultural efforts have failed.

Our knowledge of the external world and our ability to represent the world as it is or as we would like it to be has grown enormously, but our ability to meet wisely the challenge of how to be human beings has not developed equally. Everyone acknowledges this intellectually; yet no one has accepted the full implications which this failure entails for education. The Art and Science of being a Human Being is still an assignment for which the Human Race is inadequately prepared.

The failure of education to make it possible for Man to change is due to a specific component in human nature: to wit, that psychological rigidity which is the most basic and most universal expression of the neurotic process—far more universal than are those more obvious quirks which comprise the clinical neuroses. Indeed, this neurotogenic rigidity is so universal that it is popularly accepted as normal even among many psychiatrists and analysts, as though the mere fact that everybody is rigid in one or more aspects of his personality meant that rigidity is normal. Cavities in the teeth are not normal merely because everybody has cavities. Nor is a cold normal because everybody catches cold. Actually, this psychological rigidity, which is a manifestation of the masked but universal neurotic ingredient in human nature, constitutes the major challenge not only to education but to any general forward movement on the part of human culture.

(2) Since all that I will say is predicated upon what I regard as this basic failure of human culture, I must enumerate the indices of this failure, even if in doing so I repeat part of what I have already said:

First there is the universality of the neurotic process itself, in every culture about which we know anything. From one society to another there are minor variations in the forms in which the neurotic process manifests itself. Yet the universality of its essence is attested by its appearance in these varied forms among peoples from all cultures.

Second, there is the basic failure of the race as a whole, plus the failure of men as individuals, to evolve and change psychologically.

Third, there is the failure of traditional methods of imparting that wisdom about living which would be manifest in socially creative and individually fulfilling lives of work and play and love. We dare not pretend to ourselves that we have solved this problem. Thus we know what kinds of behavioral conventions tend to conserve any association of men in a livable society. We call these ethical principles. Yet we cannot claim that we know how to perpetuate and inculcate such ethical principles, or how to seat them firmly in the saddle in human affairs. Instead we know that out of unsavory soil some people grow up to be ethical, while others become unethical from equivalently favored circumstances. The son of a criminal may become a minister: and the son of a minister, a criminal. Or if we take marriage as another example, the progeny from happy marriages may make unhappy unions, and vice versa: just as happens in the careers of the sons of "great" men or of failures. Clearly there are basic gaps in our knowledge of how to transmit the fruits of experience from one generation to the next. The consequence is that in forms which change only in details, country after country and generation after generation repeat the errors of their predecessors.

The cumulative significance of these interdependent manifestations of the failure of culture is to place at the heart of our problem the universal masked neurotic components in "normal" human nature. Therefore, we must ask ourselves whether the educational process as we know it increases or decreases in the student the incidence and the sway of hidden neurotic forces in human life.

Education and the Neurotic Process

It is often said that one could not get through school at all without a neurosis of some degree and kind. The neurosis which is implied here is the "compulsive work drive." Yet compulsive drives are not a separate clinical entity; since there is a compulsive nucleus in all manifestations of the neurotic process. Furthermore, even if this has been true in the past (which has certainly seemed to be the case for graduate professional schools), it need not always be our fate. But it is with the defects of the present that we must concern ourselves, if we are to reach a better future. Therefore it is this unhappy symbiosis between education and the ubiquitous neurotic process that we must consider.

Obviously, every man is a pupil for many years before he attains the state of being an adult with more or less independent fields of activity. Just as we carry over into adult life the distortions which arise in the nursery, so we carry into our adult years the stresses and strains of our educational adolescence: i.e., the years during which we struggle to acquire knowledge, craftsmanship, technique, and discrimination. Whether he becomes an artist, a scientist, a professional man, a postman, a plumber, or a salesman, the adult bears the imprint of the child. The unconscious projection of the years of childhood onto the screen of adult years limits our capacity to mature by anchoring us to the past. Therefore, the educator who is interested in making education serve the process of maturity must study the ways in which such projections from the past influence four elements in education, i.e.:

(1) the *setting* in which we impart education;

(2) the *methods* by which we teach and learn;

(3) the *data* which we try to impart;

(4) the *symbolic process*.

(1) *The Setting of Education: and its Influence on the Neurotic Process.* The schoolroom and the school as a whole confront the child with surrogate parents and siblings. If we were naïvely optimistic we might expect that schools would long since have seized on this as an opportunity to explore each child's responses both to parental authority and to sibling rivalry, so as to help him to understand himself in these basic relationships and thus to achieve a capacity for mature self-direction. Instead, in most schools the structure of school "society" is such as to allow the child merely to relive blindly the buried hates and loves and fears and rivalries which had

their origins at home—sacrificing understanding to some limited degree of blind "self-mastery." Schooling tends rather to accentuate whatever automatic patterns of child-to-adult and child-to-child relationship each child has brought to his school years, and not to change them. The schoolroom as we know it tends neither to balance nor to neutralize these conflict-laden feelings, nor to render them less fixed and rigid by bringing them within the reach of conscious selection, direction, and control. Self-control as taught is limited to a control of the secondary consequence of these conflicts, never directed at their inner sources. The exceptions to this are rare. At best, most schools today constitute a pragmatic test of the extent to which a student as he comes to them can either accept or reject or modify or exercise authority.

One could choose at random a number of illustrations of the consequences of this. First among them is the child who in his struggle with authority becomes an obsessional dawdler. This may begin in the nursery in dawdling about eating, excreting, washing, dressing, or undressing. Such a toddler grows up to be an obsessional dawdler about play, chores, and studies. As we have said, the school patterns of young lives do not arise de novo, but carry the imprint of a nursery prehistory which antedated schooling. One phase merges into the next. Consequently, unless these earlier neurotic deviations have been effectively resolved in the home before the youngster reaches school, they will invade and warp his later approach to study of all kinds.

Yet the school does nothing to give the child either insight into them or freedom from them. Instead it usually increases this paralyzing tendency, so that the same patterns will persist to plague the lifework of potentially brilliant and creative adults. It is in this way that the deviations of each untreated phase are accentuated in later phases, and gather new and increasingly costly secondary consequences. One can trace this story in many lives.

For some the only escape from this prison is to turn away from all formal and informal education, rejecting any guidance from the past, and from those products of Man's experience which are embodied in "rules" or "principles." This is a not infrequent source of the undisciplined, chaotic, and rebellious pseudo-creativity which characterizes the early work of many young artists, writers, musicians, and scientists. As children many of them had been paralyzed by the obsessional dawdling which is a carry-over from nursery years. In the effort to escape, they grow up to accept unwittingly the tyranny of an internal "Führer" of which they are unaware. They are seduced by the illusory freedom of a blind reaction against all *external* authority. Yet because the road to freedom is never found by submitting to irresponsible authority (whether this authority is internal or external), inevitably they pay for this in the stereotyped and repetitive quality of their work. Such creativity wears only a mask of freedom. All too often their continued enslavement becomes manifest in a crippling work-block, and in years of total unproductivity which may engulf and paralyze even great creative artists. (Cf., for instance, Sterba, 73, De Voto, 11.)

At the opposite pole from the obsessional dawdler is the compulsive rusher, the youngster who has to plunge headlong from one half-finished task to another, afraid to tarry long enough to complete anything lest he be over-taken by some nameless fate, some dreaded exposure. These two oppositely paced obligatory patterns may alternate in the same individual, and may arise out of almost identical neurotic soil, that is to say, out of essentially identical unconscious conflicts. Yet in later life these will have dramatically different secondary and tertiary consequences. The relevant and disconcerting point is that both of these opposing neurotic patterns tend to be reinforced and not lessened by the pressures of our formal educational processes.

Consider also the influence of the educational setting on another pair of neurotic mechanisms. The "bad" student explodes in automatic defiance, with the repression of all latent compliant impulses. In the so-called "good" student, whose "goodness" may be equally automatic, the same struggle is often buried in neurotic submissiveness, with the repression of all latent rebellion. This is one of several reasons why every analyst has a category of patients who can best be called "Campus Heroes," i.e., men and women who have done extraordinarily well through school and college on the basis of a neurotic submissiveness, which ultimately explodes in their forties and fifties under the pressure of unresolved underlying problems.

Such clinical experiences as these challenge us to ask whether there is any better way to conduct the educational process, which will free it on the one hand from the subtle distortions of neurotic submissiveness with its unimaginative conformity, and on the other from unconscious rebellion with its pseudo-originality; and also from the diffuse blocking which can be a manifestation of unconscious sabotage and of other neurotogenic inhibitory constellations.

The accepted settings of education reinforce still other neurotogenic sequences. For instance, the classroom perpetuates on every level the struggle within each generation, as well as between child and adult. This happens because most schools still exploit competitively the hostilities and the sibling rivalries which arise automatically in every nursery. Almost never are these resolved or illuminated in the classroom with insight, grace, or compassion. Consequently a competitive rivalry occurs which can overstimulate one student and overinhibit another. I have seen this happen with disastrous consequences to two pairs of identical twins. In each of these one of the pair was overstimulated and the other overinhibited by reliving in the schoolroom the sibling situation at home. Here again are destructive forms in which the classroom can constitute a screen upon which the bitter, hidden residues of earlier years can be projected into the child's present and the adult's future. This is one of the prices our culture pays for the failure of schools to use the classroom as an opportunity to resolve these corroding conflicts.

In considering how to deal with these difficult and ubiquitous problems we do not need to conjure up a Utopian School in which no nursery battles would be re-enacted. As a guiding principle we need only remember that the immediate and the remote effects of these internal and external sources of conflict upon each child and adult will depend not upon the fact that these struggles occur, but upon the level on which they are waged, i.e., whether this level is preponderantly conscious, preconscious, or unconscious. Therefore we can justly challenge our schools to see what they can do to make sure that these battles will be fought out on conscious and preconscious levels. With this reasonable and attainable goal in mind, they could use the classroom replications of infancy as an opportunity to develop in each child at least that degree of self-knowledge which would be sufficient to free him from passive submission to the tyranny of his ancient and submerged patterns. It would seem to be an essential ingredient of any truly educational experience to enable each child to face in himself those painful conflicts from which he shrinks but which shape his character. Instead, it has been the traditionally accepted role of the school to impose even stronger taboos on self-knowledge than are generated at home, thus reinforcing and reproducing in the classroom the very limitations on self-awareness which characterize our adult culture. Thus what passes for Education strengthens that all-too-human tendency to shrink from the facing of painful facts, which the child brings to school from his nursery.

Neither traditional disciplinary education nor progressive education has solved the technical problems which this goal involves; although progressive education has launched a courageous if sometimes blind struggle towards their solution. Disciplinary techniques alone, even when seemingly "successful," give the child a sense that he must control something, but fail to make clear what there is inside to control or redirect. Especially in its early years, "progressive" education encouraged the child to act out his problems, but failed to realize that acting-out will not alone bring any increase in self-understanding or in self-mastery. Indeed, like blind discipline, blind acting-out can distort and block insight; as we see in the psychopath. This fallacy was manifested in the misapplication to education of a procedure which is valid in therapy, but even there only under certain circumstances. It was not strange that in its early stages progressive education should have made this mistake. This error has long been abandoned; but without finding what to put in its place. About this I will presently make a few tentative suggestions.

(2) *The Influence of the Techniques of Education on the Neurotic Process.* We must next ask ourselves how often traditional teaching methods distort the education even of highly gifted youngsters, (a) blocking these youngsters by intensifying the activity of inhibiting neurotic forces, or (b) overdriving them by masked neurotic obsessions and compulsions. In other words, does the educative process, even at its current best, tend to reinforce the neurotic process? I believe that it has precisely this effect, and primarily through the misuse of the techniques of repetitive drill.

In the tangled interweaving of the processes of learning and the neurotic process, repetition plays a major role. By imperceptible gradations, the repetitive drills of the learning process shade over into the automatic involuntary repetitions of the neurosis. But whenever repetition becomes automatic and obligatory, it constitutes the kernel of the neurotic process itself. Unhappily this is precisely what often occurs in education, with the consequence that an intensification of the neurotic process through repetitive drill mars our educational system from primary grades through professional and graduate levels.

This neurotic distortion of repetitive drill in the learning process can frustrate the practice of the athlete, of the musician, of the student of languages, of mathematics, of history, of the young scientist, indeed of any effort to memorize or master anything. As a consequence of this contamination of the learning process by neurotic automaticity, repetitive drill makes imperfect at least as frequently (and probably far more frequently) than it makes perfect. It grinds in error and makes more "bad habits" than good. If this were not true, practice would turn all of us into virtuosi, champion athletes, and TV quiz experts.

These facts are observable every day in every home and every school. Limitless repetition without the guidance of insight is not merely self-defeating; it does deeper damage by hampering spontaneous, "intuitive," i.e., preconscious functions. There is considerable evidence that the freer is the learning process from neurotic distortion, and the less obstructed it is by counter-processes which are rooted in unconscious conflicts (i.e., the more "normal" it is), the less repetition is needed. Nevertheless in the acquisition of any skills, whether manipulative, symbolic, or instinctive, the teacher continues to place major emphasis on repetitive drill.

The most efficient learning is essentially effortless and almost instantaneous. This is that preconscious learning, to which the closest analogy is the automatic and almost photographic or phonographic hypermnesia of hypnosis. For example, under hypnosis enormous amounts of material can be recorded effortlessly, almost as on a photographic plate. Here drill and repetition play no role; and their introduction would actually interfere with automatic recording. This is true whether the learn-ing process is predominantly visual, auditory, manipula-tive, or kinesthetic, although there may be differences in inherent endowments in this respect. In general, how-ever, the degree to which learning depends upon repeti-tive drill is a measure of the degree to which guilt, anxiety, anger, and repression, whether conscious or unconscious, are blocking the assimilative component of education. Thus dependence on drill is actually a measure of the failure of at least one important ingredient in the educa-tional process, while reflecting the influence of the edu-cator's anxiety as well. The result is to increase the en-tanglement of preconscious functions in a thicket of un-conscious guilt, terror, rage, and conflict. An illuminating contrast is provided by the "idiot-savant," a person of limited mentality who functions so nearly free of conflict as to be able to record preconsciously as though under hypnosis, and thus is able to produce extraordinary feats of memory, of lightning calculation, etc. Occasionally one encounters a man or child whose preconscious learn-ing processes, through some happy accident, operate freely. He learns effortlessly. To the consternation and anger of his classmates he wins highest grades in a heavy schedule without studying. Yet because he has done this with Seven League Boots, and at the speed of all precon-scious processes and without laboring through the inter-mediate steps, he is unable to explain to anyone else how he has done it. Nor can he teach. Similarly the great vir-tuosi and the greatest athletes are rarely the great teachers.

(3) *The Influence of Unconscious Projection on the Materials to be Mastered in the Educative Process.* There is another technical aspect of education which points up

its interrelation with the neurotic process. The learning process is a continuous two-way interchange. It has acquisitive elements insofar as it involves the assimilation of new data. Yet at the same time every new thing that we attempt to assimilate becomes a target for projections, comparable to the projections which are demonstrated in the Rorschach Test, the Thematic Apperception Test, the Zondi tests, etc. William James characterized this many years ago when he said that every Perception requires a prior Apperceptive act: i.e., the integration of the data of the preceptual process into a mass of previously acquired data which he called the "apperceptive mass." Freud restated this when he said that every Cognition implies a process of Recognition.

Whenever the eager student undertakes to master a new discipline, its special data are at first amorphous and structureless. Each new discipline is like a cinema screen onto which each student projects representations of his own unresolved unconscious problems. In this way we first distort what we attempt to learn, and then learn what we have distorted. Everything that we study undergoes this double process and acquires multiple significance: (a) There is the process of perceiving and of apperceiving new facts and new combinations of facts, leading to new concepts. (b) Paralleling this, we continuously project onto this material distillates of our own unconscious psychological processes. This occurs whether we are studying literature, the arts, music, languages, or mathematics, the sciences, history, philosophy—anything. Through such projections onto the subject matter of various disciplines, as we master them the disciplines themselves are converted into complex, challenging thematic apperceptive devices.

Presumably, this process of projection must play a major role among the several forces which determine a man's choice of his occupation or of fields for study and research. Vocational choices have never been studied from this angle. Yet this type of distortion, which plagues the educational process, can itself be made the object of research by techniques which are available to us, but which have never been used for this purpose. This, however, is not the occasion for a discussion of details of research into the educative process.

(4) *Symbolic Distortions.* A further difficulty in educational procedures which is related to these projective experiences arises through the neurotic distortion of the symbolic process itself. Of this the most obvious and universal manifestation is the dream; but in subtler form the same thing occurs in learning. The symbolic process always represents a condensation of conscious, preconscious, and unconscious symbolic values. In elementary learning quite as much as in the higher levels of research, there can be a subtle and unnoticed shift from the conscious import of anything to its unconscious connotations. In turn this can initiate blindly compulsive workdrives in unprofitable directions. One encounters this repeatedly in the lives of scientists, artists, and writers. Alternatively it may set up equally blind resistances to the processes of learning, resistances which may be either selective or all-inclusive. It is in this way that the symbolic process can become an obstacle to the learning process instead of its chief tool.

Thus, at every level of education from the kindergarten to postgraduate study, educational procedures become intricate networks of normal and neurotic mechanisms. Moreover, because as we have seen, traditional techniques of teaching employ mechanisms similar to those which dominate the neurotic process, education itself involves a subtle trend towards neurotic distortion, the correction of which demands a continuous use of clinically appropriate preventive devices. People talk glibly of neuroses as a kind of mal-education and of psychotherapy as a process of learning. Both statements are oversimplifications, slighting and overlooking among other considerations the basic fact that conventional educational techniques exploit and depend upon some of the essential ingredients of the neurotic process. The consequence is that one cannot dissociate an unsparing study of how to improve the learning processes from the understanding and control of neurotic mechanisms. Therapy and learning constitute together a joint field for research in education and psychiatry. Therefore, education and therapy are complementary and inseparable.[2]

From all of these considerations we are forced to conclude that there is a continuous conflict and not a happy synergy between erudition and maturity. This conflict begins in the primary grades but continues unabated to and through the highest echelons of postgraduate education.

---

[2] Two articles not otherwise related to the theme of these lectures trace this intricate interlacing of the neurotic and educative processes, and point out that they are one of several considerations which call for the development of a new profession, i.e., a doctorate in Medical Psychology, standing halfway between the psychiatrist and the clinical psychologist as we know them today. Cf. L. S. Kubie, "The Pros and Cons of a New Profession: A Doctorate in Medical Psychology," from *Texas Reports on Biology and Medicine*, 12 (No. 3), 692-737; reprinted in "Medical and Psychological Teamwork in the Care of the Chronically Ill," chapter V, pp. 125-169, Harrower, M. (ed.), Thomas, Springfield, Ill., 1955; and L. S. Kubie, "The Need for a New Sub-discipline in the Medical Profession," *Archives of Neurology and Psychiatry*, 1 (September, 1957), 283-293.

Erudition without Wisdom or Maturity

I have never been able to regard seriously any partisan arguments that the study of any particular aspect of man's folly-ridden history will determine whether the scholar ends up with mature wisdom or with the pseudo-erudition of an idiot-savant. The conflict between education as we have known it and maturity as we can envisage it depends upon something more profound than whether we master the history of an art-form called painting or of an art-form called science. There is no educator who does not know scholars who lack the least quality of human maturity and wisdom, yet who are true masters of their own fields, whether this field is the humanities, art, music, philosophy, religion, law, science, the history of ideas or the languages by which men communicate ideas. The absent-minded professor may be a stereotype, a burlesque, and an exaggeration; but he symbolizes a remoteness from wisdom and maturity which demonstrates that there is no degree of learning about the phenomenology of the outer world or about the histories of *other* lands, *other* peoples, and *other* men's lives, which in and of itself brings wisdom. The absent-minded professor, whatever his field, is the living proof that the scholarly humanist is not necessarily wiser by virtue of his special knowledge than is the technical scientist, or vice versa. Indeed nowadays we are all technicians. The measure of our wisdom about living is not determined by the breadth of our knowledge, or by the sharpness of the focus of our specialization.

If only as a contrast, it might shed some light on the elusive relationship between formal education and maturation to consider what happens to medical students during the course of their medical education. All close observers agree that it has a remarkable impact on many, if not on all. Furthermore, this critical change seems to start not when the students are studying books or dissecting corpses or working in laboratories, but when they are brought into contact with the sufferings of patients. This is a moment which forces them to accept some measure of responsibility for human suffering other than their own. For each student this is an experience which precipitates a powerful if masked internal struggle among conflicting impulses. Shall he or shall he not be his brother's keeper? Shall he cling to the unrecognized prerogative of childhood to shut out the suffering of others or even secretly to exult in it? Or shall he yield to those simultaneous, powerful, internal and external pressures which medical tradition brings to bear on him, to force a confrontation with human needs other than his own? Will this extricate him from the cocoon of his childhood to identify with others through ministering to them?

This may give us a clue to another basic defect in our entire educational process. Perhaps above anything else the adolescent needs not only to be exposed to human suffering, but also to be given responsibility to play a role in ministering to it. At present the educational years cultivate in each student a maximal concentration on himself. One can conjure up many methods by which this problem might at least be explored.[3]

---

[3] Today one of the significant experiments in this direction is going on at the George Junior Republic. Consider also the Civilian Conservation Corps of the years of the great depression, and also the National Service Fraternity known as Alpha Phi Omega.

The difficulty is intensified by the fact that the increasing duration of education competes with the equally essential needs of young men and women for experience and responsibility. We know that the essence of maturity can come only through the insight which arises out of the interaction between living, blundering, and studying and dissecting our blunders. Neither living without self-study, nor study without living is enough. We sometimes forget that the founders of the Republic lived and also often died young—and that in their moment of national greatness many were only in their thirties. Yet this is precisely where the rub is; because the increasing duration of the process of formal education tends to incarcerate the student for many decades in an adolescence of limited responsibility in which he lives on a dole, thus obstructing the very processes of maturation for which we are striving. The effort to educate fully may take so many years that it can make unattainable the very development at which it aims. The persistent immaturity of the perpetual student is a familiar phenomenon on every campus; and when any training program lasts too long, independent spirits tend to drop out along the way, until only the docile, the submissive, and the uncreative survive the full indoctrination. We face this problem in all forms of education. How to achieve the fullest degree of intellectual preparation without emotional stunting challenges us to find ways in which without limiting education we can facilitate those aspects of emotional maturity which emanate only from the direct experience of living and from carrying a sobering responsibility for others.

I take it for granted that our educational processes must continue to last longer and longer. This means, however, that unless the student is exposed concurrently to maturing experiences, he will continue to end up as an erudite adolescent. The mere passage of time makes maturity possible, but never guarantees it. Without the challenge of independent responsibility (personal, professional, and/or clinical), the duration of training tends to limit the emotional maturation which is a vital component in the equipment of anyone who hopes to achieve wisdom.

Precisely here is where the educational system, the neurotic process, and the emotional demands of the creative impulse come into a three-way collision. For reasons which I have tried to indicate, the imperious creative impulse frequently arises in a young man or woman who is rebelling against all external authority, yet who has unwittingly remained enslaved to his own unconscious. He brooks no external interference: but also will not welcome any well-meant efforts on the part of others to help him to become free from the internal slave-driver about whose existence he is both unconscious and paradoxically defensive. Therefore he rejects not only formal educational responsibility but also any depths of self-understanding. Thus he turns his back on both types of potentially maturing experience to which the human spirit can be exposed. He will not wait humbly for the wisdom that can be won only at the "autopsy table," i.e., through the study of his own errors, which is the only path we know to self-knowledge in depth. His rebellious spirit may instead seize upon his own particular field of art or music or literature or science, to use it as a vehicle for aggressive expression of his own neurosis.

As with all Priesthoods this is to him a "calling" of sorts; and like all "callings" it feeds on the fantasy that he can create out of revelation. In one field the revelations are absolute truths from a Deity. In another they arise out of some secret wellspring of Absolutes from within. Out of this unconscious arrogance has grown the unspoken Dogma that ignorance in the creative artist should be cultivated as a positive advantage, so as to leave him unencumbered by reality. Yet curiously enough, as with all such notions, it contains a minute grain of truth.

One obvious implication runs through everything I have said, namely, that if education is to become a matter not only of the mind but of the spirit, and that if it is ever to facilitate the maturing process instead of limiting and distorting it, then it must deal with the universal, masked, neurotic ingredient in human nature. Clearly this will require an unsparing reappraisal of all traditional educational goals and methods. This leads me to my final argument.

3. THE ROLE OF SELF-KNOWLEDGE

These are grave facts to be pondered gravely by every educator. You will understand why I began by stating that I have no easy solutions. Nevertheless as I draw to a close I will urge that one thing is an essential ingredient in any solution. This is self-knowledge in depth (48, 49).

Thus far my ruminations have merely led me up to the brink of this critical question: namely, what is the effective value of knowledge of externals in the absence of equally deep personal insight? Can there be wisdom, even about the objective world around us (considering how many distorting fantasies we project onto this outer world) in the absence of wisdom about the inner world from which these projections arise? It is my conviction that education without self-knowledge can never mean wisdom or maturity; and that self-knowledge in depth is a process which like education itself is never complete. It is a point on a continuous and never-ending journey. It is always relative, and never absolute. It is a process which must go on throughout life, if at all; and like the fight for external freedom, it demands eternal vigilance and continuous struggle. This is because in every one of us, from the beginning of life until its end active forces are at work which tend repeatedly to confuse and obscure our images of ourselves. Therefore, that well-known average man who lacks self-knowledge in depth, looks out upon the world through glasses which are discolored by the quality of his own unconscious self-image. Without self-knowledge in depth we can have dreams, but no art. We can have the neurotic raw material of literature but not mature literature. We can have no adults, but only aging children who are armed with words and paint and clay and atomic weapons, none of which they understand. And the greater the role in the educational process which is played by unconscious components of symbolic thinking, the wider must be this ancient and dishonorable gap between erudition and wisdom. It is this gap which makes a mockery of the more pretentious claims of art, of science, of education, and of religion. If self-knowledge has been the forgotten man of our educational system, and indeed of human culture in general, then we are forced to the conclusion that up to now it has been possible for men in general to be only erudite rather than wise. Wisdom when it has graced any one of us has come not by design but as a happy accident. This challenges us to have the courage to face this failure of education as we have always known it, with a determination to do something effective about it.[4]

I would not like this argument to be misunderstood or exaggerated. Self-knowledge is not all there is to wisdom and maturity; but it is an essential ingredient which makes maturity at least possible. Yet it is the one ingredient which is almost totally neglected. This lack is both an index and a cause of the immaturity of our culture.

4. Summary and Suggestions

If I now summarize these reflections, what do we find? We find ourselves confronted with a whole series of difficult paradoxes and dilemmas, and with no simple indication of how to reconcile or solve them. The amount of data which every educated man must master is enormous already and is constantly increasing. Yet if we hold him at the student level too long, the process of emotional maturation which is so essential an ingredient of education is in danger of being stunted. And as more and more must be learned, the danger of stunting will increase un-

---

[4] Even the preoccupation with other men's lives is often used to evade self-knowledge: "I believe that every student of the behavioral sciences has as the source of his basic interest in behavior a profound concern with human behavior. He may study rats or ants or fish or ducks; but this may be an unconscious obsessional defense against his psychophobia, as Lewin has called it. The possible psychophobic roots of such an interest are relevant here for only one reason. If a scientist has turned away from the direct study of man because of unconscious taboos which forbid him to look on man and woman, if to look on human behavior has acquired for this scientist some of the connotations of peeking through a keyhole, then to his surprise he will find himself unable to apply to animals the lessons and methods which he has learned from man without stirring in himself an obstructing sense of anxiety and guilt. Nor will he be able to apply to man what he learns about the lower animals. Of the stifling and blinding influence of these affective blocks on the free interchange among behavioral scientists, I could give innumerable examples" (Kubie, 48).

less we can find a way to make over the life of the student, so that in itself it will become a maturing experience.

Here again the use of what we have learned through psychoanalysis from these exaggerations of the normal which we call abnormal will play a critical role. Even if we do not already possess the techniques by which to implement fully the knowledge we have gained, we can at least formulate our goals. Education must include opportunities to undo some of those subtle restrictions of the human spirit which arise as a result of the ubiquitous if masked influence of both the neurotic and the schizophrenic processes in every culture known to man. Furthermore, in our society many active forces obstruct any effort to apply even the imperfect and incomplete knowledge which we now possess. Entrenched special interests oppose change, because they are threatened by change. Therefore, progress will not come just from sitting back and hoping, or from studying. It will come only as a reward for an uncompromising defense of the creative value of doubt, and from an unsparingly critical re-examination of every educational premise. When we meet the currently popular and all too easy assumption that the humanities will solve these problems, we should remind the optimist that the humanities have never served us that well in the past. The crucial question is not whether one should study science or the humanities, but what can be done to convert the years of the student's life into a maturing experience. Either the basic structure of that life must be altered; or else periods of study must be interspersed with periods devoted to other types of experiences; or techniques of group psychotherapy must be adapted to the educational scene to supplement formal education in the service of greater maturity. Or all of these must be tried.

The emotional and intellectual maturity which the returning veteran brought to his studies after World War II, the subtle birth of a larval maturity in the medical student as he first experiences the suffering of others and participates in its alleviation, what we have learned about the imprisoning of the human spirit by the neurotic process—these lead us in the direction in which we must seek solutions to these fundamental problems of how education can enable the human spirit to grow and change. We cannot be wise yet remain immature. Maturity requires the capacity to change, to become different, to react in varied and unanticipated ways. All of these words describe different facets of this same human need: and none of it is attainable as long as the human spirit remains imprisoned in its masked neuroses. This is the ultimate challenge to the value of any educational process in any culture.

Chapter 4

General Summary

(1) It has been my thesis that a type of mental function, which we call technically "the preconscious system," is the essential implement of all creative activity; and that unless preconscious processes can flow freely there can be no true creativity.

(2) Preconscious processes, however, never operate alone. They are under the continuous and often conflicting and distorting or obstructing influence of two other concurrent systems of symbolic functions, each of which is relatively anchored and rigid. Together the three systems constitute a spectrum with certain continuities, and at least one partial but critical discontinuity.

At one pole are the symbolic processes which we speak of as *conscious*, meaning thereby that the relation between the symbol and what it represents is intact, with the result that in this area we know most of what each symbol connotes. (We can never know *all*.)

At the other pole are the symbolic processes which we call unconscious, by which we mean that although the symbol is conscious, most of what it stands for is both unknown and inaccessible except by special methods of exploration.

(3) Conscious symbolic processes are the tool by which we communicate the bare bones of meaning to one another, by which we re-examine critically our own thinking, by which we group multiple fragments of experience into unified patterns of comparable or overlapping experiences, condense different units, rearrange

them in logical or chronological categories, and build abstractions from them.

It is important to realize that without symbolic functions on the conscious level, human psychological functions would be limited to the sensory and emotional recall of fragments of past experiences. At their most vivid, these would be approximately analogous to the phenomena of the "phantom limb" (in which the sensory impressions of prior experiences are condensed and vividly relived): analogous also to the re-experiencing of confused or vaguely overlapping fragments of visual or olfactory or auditory perceptions out of the past, in dreamlike hypnagogic reveries.

Conscious symbolic processes have their primary roots in perceptions of past external and internal experiences; but evolve through generalizations into abstractions and their symbolic representations into the coded signals which we call words. This gives them their anchorage in reality, which is essential to the major function of the conscious system. Yet at the same time this automatically limits the free imaginative play of conscious symbolic processes.

On the other hand, it is also relevant to point out that without the verbal and symbolic condensations of speech, most of us would in all probability have a much richer sensory and affective recall of past events, both within the body and without. If verbal short cuts were eliminated, our everyday memories would be imprecise; but they could have the pseudo-hallucinatory vividness of hypnagogic reveries. In some respects they would be like the violent affects which can persist after dreams, even when the dreams themselves are obliterated. . . . Thus we pay a price for the superimposition of conscious symbolic function over our more primitive sensory Gestalts, and especially when the conscious symbol is a word. This price is the attenuation of the capacity to relive past experiences as vividly as though they were recurring in the present. In this sense, thinking-back verbally is a smoke screen for that true remembering which is an affectively charged re-living.

Only poets, novelists, painters and musicians are, in varying degrees and in a fragmentary way, exceptions to this rule. Certainly in all art forms, but particularly in the plastic arts and music, where the symbolic process comes closer to the nonverbal symbolic tools of the dream, there is an effort to reactivate and revivify the sensory and emotionalized (or "gut") components of past experience (47).

(4) At the other pole are what we call unconscious symbolic processes. Here the essential fact is that the relationship of the symbol to what it represents is impaired, distorted, or actually lost (or as we say "repressed"). Furthermore, this repression cannot be lifted by any simple act of will. The iron curtain between the symbol and all that it represents cannot be penetrated; and we cannot become conscious of the symbolic meanings without special techniques, such as psychoanalysis, hypnosis, certain drugs, electrical processes, various chemical changes, etc. In other words, within the unconscious system the true connotations of the symbol are inaccessible even on need to our most intent, deliberate, conscious self-inspection. Moreover in the unconscious system this relationship cannot be altered by any influences until and unless it is brought out into the open. The symbol is

to its unconscious root like a delegate who has been sent to the conference table to "negotiate," but with secret orders never to modify his position. He pretends to interchange with those who sit around the table; but his secret orders are unalterable and his ultimate position will be precisely what it was at the beginning. Similarly within the unconscious system the relationship of symbols to what they represent is impervious to conscious or preconscious experiences, with the result that it is, if anything, even more fixed and rigid than is the relation of the symbol to what it stands for in the conscious system.

The influence of this rigidity can be observed in the stereotyped repetitiousness of form and content in the works of the musician, of the artist, of the writer, and of the scientist. How often is it said that a man has painted the same painting over and over again, written the same poem, told the same story, composed the same music, ground the same scientific ax? Were it not for this fact, it would be impossible for the specialist in the arts to recognize a man's paintings from their technique and content, or his music without having been told who the composer was. It is the artist's unconscious which leaves a personal signature on his work as on his handwriting; and like a fingerprint left by a thief in the night, it is unmodifiable and therefore non-creative. This accounts also for the man who produces one play, one book, one poem, one painting, one piece of first-rate scientific work.

All of this is the price we pay whenever unconscious processes hold the upper hand in the dynamic unstable equilibrium among the CS, PCS, UCS systems during our creative efforts. The dread which haunts every creative person that this fate may be his is a product of some measure of imprecise insight into the fact that the creative potential of his preconscious processes will be captured, imprisoned, nullified, sterilized, and stereotyped by his own unconscious, i.e., by that very unconscious which paradoxically he defends desperately against any therapeutic intrusion or modification.

(5) Whence then comes our creative function? To answer this we have to stop for a moment to indicate what we mean by creativity. Clearly, by the creative process we mean the capacity to find new and unexpected connections, to voyage freely over the seas, to happen on America as we seek new routes to India, to find new relationships in time and space, and thus new meanings. Or to put it in another way, it means working freely with conscious and preconscious metaphor, with slang, puns, overlapping meanings, and figures of speech, with vague similarities, with the reminiscent recollections evoked by some minute ingredients of experience, establishing links to something else which in other respects may be quite different. It is free in the sense that it is not anchored either to the pedestrian realities of our conscious symbolic processes, or to the rigid symbolic relationships of the unconscious areas of the personality.

This is precisely why the free play of preconscious symbolic processes is vital for all creative productivity. Preconscious psychological functions stand on the fringes of consciousness. Here the meaning of the symbol is essentially analogic, yet relatively transparent, although it may be obfuscated in varying degrees for artistic purposes, as in the more obscure realms of modern art, modern verse, and modern music. Yet preconscious processes involve much more than all of this. They are also the most

141

important economizing device which implements our thinking operations.

The price that we pay for traditional educational methods is that they either tie our preconscious symbolic processes prematurely to precise realities, or leave them to the mercy of distorting influences which arise around areas of unresolved unconscious conflict.

Together all of this carries the implication that the ad hoc postulate that there is a separate and special mechanism known as the sublimation of unconscious processes may not be needed to explain creativity, and may actually be misleading. This concept was formulated as an effort to explain creativity in relation to neurotic conflicts *before* the role of the preconscious system, its speed, its versatility, its brilliance, and its vulnerability were fully appreciated. The concept of sublimation, natural though it may have been, is based on inaccurate assumptions about the energetics of psychological processes (55). Furthermore the concept carries the impossible connotation that unconscious conflicts can be resolved if they can be expressed in socially valuable forms instead of in useless or destructive forms. Yet no compulsive work drive has ever healed itself through working, however successfully.

These considerations lead to a few conclusions:

(1) Neurosis corrupts, mars, distorts, and blocks creativeness in every field.

(2) No one need fear that getting well will cause an atrophy of his creative drive.

(3) This illusory fear rests on the erroneous assumption that it is that which is unconscious in us which makes us creative, whereas in fact the unconscious is our

straitjacket, rendering us as stereotyped and as sterile and as repetitive as is the neurosis itself.

(4) Where unconscious influences play a dominant role the creative process in science or art becomes almost identical with the neurotic process—merely transmuting unconscious conflicts into some socially and artistically acceptable symbolic form.

(5) The goal to seek is to free preconscious processes from the distortions and obstructions interposed by unconscious processes and from the pedestrian limitations of conscious processes. The unconscious can spur it on. The conscious can criticize and correct and evaluate. But creativity is a product of preconscious activity. This is the challenge which confronts the education of the future.

Works Cited

1. ALSCHULER, ROSE H., and HATTWICK, LA BERTA WEISS, *Painting and Personality, a Study of Young Children*, Chicago, Illinois, 1947.
2. BABBITT, IRVING, *On Being Creative*, Boston and New York, 1932.
3. BERNARD, CLAUDE, *An Introduction to the Study of Experimental Medicine*, tr. Greene, H. G., New York, 1927.
4. BLACKMUR, R. P., *Anni Mirabiles 1921-1925—Reason in the Madness of Letters* (four lectures presented under the Gertrude Clarks Whittall Poetry and Literature Fund, January, 1956, Library of Congress Lecture Series), Washington, D.C.
5. BOAS, GEORGE, (a) *Philosophy and Poetry*, Norton, Massachusetts, 1932.
6. BOAS, GEORGE, (b) "An Eightfold Confusion in Aesthetic Evaluations," *Modern Language Notes*, XLVIII (February, 1933), 69-80.
7. BOAS, GEORGE, (c) "What is a Picture?" *The Johns Hopkins Magazine*, VIII (December, 1956), 8-13.
8. CANE, FLORENCE, *The Artist in Each of Us*, New York, 1951.
9. CANE, MELVILLE, *Making a Poem—An Inquiry into the Creative Process*, New York, 1953.
10. DEVOTO, BERNARD, "Freud in American Literature," *Psychoanalytic Quarterly*, IX (1940), 236-245.
11. DEVOTO, BERNARD, *Mark Twain at Work*, Cambridge, Mass., 1942.
12. ERICKSON, MILTON, HUSTON, PAUL E., and SHAKOW, DAVID, "A Study of Hypnotically Induced Complexes by Means of the Luria Technique," *Journal of General Pyschology*, II (1934), 65-97.
13. ERICKSON, MILTON, "Experimental Demonstrations of the Psychopathology of Everyday Life," *Psychonanalytic Quarterly*, VIII (1939), 338-353.
14. FISCHER, CHARLES, "Dreams, Images, and Perception," *Journal of the American Psychoanalytic Association*, IV (No. 1) (January, 1956), 5-48.
15. FREUD, SIGMUND, *The Psychopathology of Everyday Life*, first published in 1914; republished (15th edition) by the Macmillan Company in 1930.

16. FREUD, SIGMUND, *Leonardo da Vinci: A Study in Sexuality*, tr. Brill, A. A., New York, 1916; republished by Random House, New York, 1947.

17. FREUD, SIGMUND, *Delusion and Dream—An Interpretation in the Light of Psychoanalysis of Gradiva, a novel by Wilhelm Jensen*, tr. Downey, Helen M., introduction by Hall, G. Stanley, New York, 1917; London, 1921.

18. FREUD, SIGMUND, *Dostoevski: Stavrogin's Confession—Suppressed Chapters from "The Possessed,"* tr. Woolf, Virginia, and Koteliansky, S. S., with a psychoanalytic study of the author, New York, 1947.

19. GHISELIN, BREWSTER, *The Creative Process: A Symposium*, Berkeley and Los Angeles, 1954.

20. GOITEIN, LIONEL, *Art and the Unconscious*, United Book Guild, 1948.

21. GREENACRE, PHYLLIS, "The Mutual Adventures of Jonathan Swift and Lemuel Gulliver," *Psychoanalytic Quarterly*, XXIV (1955), 21-62.

22. GREGG, ALAN, *The Furtherance of Medical Research*, New Haven, 1941.

23. HADAMARD, JACQUES, *The Psychology of Invention in the Mathematical Field*, Princeton, 1945.

24. HIRSCH, NATHANIEL D. M., *Genius and Creative Intelligence*, Cambridge, Mass., 1931.

25. HITSCHMANN, EDWARD, *Great Men: Psychoanalytic Studies*, New York, 1956.

26. HOFFMAN, FREDERICK J., *Freudianism and the Literary Mind*, Baton Rouge, 1945.

27. JONES, ERNEST, *Nightmares, Witches and Devils*, New York, 1931.

28. KRIS, ERNST, *Psychoanalytic Explorations in Art*, New York, 1952.

29. KUBIE, LAWRENCE S., "An Analysis of *God's Little Acre* by Caldwell, T.," *Saturday Review of Literature*, XI (1934), 305-306, 312.

30. KUBIE, LAWRENCE S., "Body Symbolization and the Development of Language," *Psychoanalytic Quarterly*, III (1934), 430-444.

31. KUBIE, LAWRENCE S., "Relation of the Conditioned Reflex to Psychoanalytic Technique," *Archives of Neurology and Psychiatry*, XXXII (1934), 1137-1142.

32. KUBIE, LAWRENCE S., "The Literature of Horror: An Analysis of *Sanctuary* by Faulkner, William," *Saturday Review of Literature*, XI (1934), 218, 224-226.

33. Kubie, Lawrence S. and Erickson, M. H., "The Use of Automatic Drawing in the Interpretation and Relief of a State of Acute Obsessional Depression," *Psychoanalytic Quarterly*, VII (1938), 443-466.

34. Kubie, Lawrence S., "The Experimental Induction of Neurotic Reactions in Man," *Yale Journal of Biology and Medicine*, II (1939), 541-545.

35. Kubie, Lawrence S., "The Repetitive Core of the Neurosis," *Psychoanalytic Quarterly*, X (1941), 23-43.

36. Kubie, Lawrence S., Margolin, Sydney G., Stone, L., and Kanzer, M., "Acute Emotional Disturbances in Torpedoed Seamen of the Merchant Marine Who Are Continuing at Sea," *War Medicine*, III (1943), 393-408.

37. Kubie, Lawrence S., "Manual of Emergency Treatment for Acute War Neuroses," *War Medicine*, IV (1943), 582-598.

38. Kubie, Lawrence S., and Margolin, Sydney G., "A Neurosis in a Merchant Seaman," *Journal of Abnormal and Social Psychology*, XXXIX (No. 2) (1944), 1-9.

39. Kubie, Lawrence S., and Margolin, Sydney G., "The Process of Hypnotism and the Nature of the Hypnotic State," *American Journal of Psychiatry*, C (1944), 611-622.

40. Kubie, Lawrence S., "The Value of Induced Dissociated States in the Therapeutic Process," *Proceedings of the Royal Society of Medicine*, London, XXXVIII (1945), 681-683.

41. Kubie, Lawrence S., Bartemeier, L. H., and others, "Combat Exhaustion," *Journal of Nervous and Mental Disease*, CIV (October, 1946), 358-389; and CIV (November, 1946), 489-525.

42. Kubie, Lawrence S., "The Psychiatrist Considers Curriculum Development," *Teachers' College Record*, L (1949), 241-246; reprinted in *Educational Psychology*, ed. Coladarci, A. P., New York, Chap. 7, Part 36, pp. 527-534.

43. Kubie, Lawrence S., *Practical and Theoretical Aspects of Psychoanalysis*, New York, 1950.

44. Kubie, Lawrence S., "The Relationship of Symbolic Function to Language Formation and to the Neurosis," *Transactions of the Seventh Conference on Cybernetics*, pp. 209-235, ed. Von Foerster, H., Josiah Macy Jr. Foundation, New York, 1950.

45. KUBIE, LAWRENCE S., "Problems and Techniques of Psychoanalytic Validation and Progress," Hixon Fund Lectures of the California Institute of Technology on *Psychoanalysis as Science*, pp. 46-124, ed. Pumpian-Mindlin, E., Stanford University Press, California, 1952.

46. KUBIE, LAWRENCE S., "Concept of Normality and Neurosis," in *Psychoanalysis and Social Work*, Chap. I, pp. 3-14, ed. Heiman, M., New York, 1953.

47. KUBIE, LAWRENCE S., "The Distortion of the Symbolic Process in Neurosis and Psychosis," *Journal of the American Psychoanalytic Association*, I (1953), 59-86.

48. KUBIE, LAWRENCE S., "Some Unsolved Problems of the Scientific Career," *American Scientist*, XLI (October, 1953), 596-613; and XLII (January, 1954), 104-112.

49. KUBIE, LAWRENCE S., "The Forgotten Man of Education," *Harvard Alumni Bulletin*, LVI (1954), 349-353.

50. KUBIE, LAWRENCE S., "The Fundamental Nature of the Distinction between Normality and Neurosis," *Psychoanalytic Quarterly*, XXIII (1954), 167-204.

51. KUBIE, LAWRENCE S., "Freud and Human Freedom," *Saturday Review*, XXXIX (May, 1956), 9-10, 36-37.

52. KUBIE, LAWRENCE S., "The Influence of Symbolic Processes on the Role of Instincts in Human Behavior," *Psychosomatic Medicine*, XVIII (May-June, 1956), 189-208.

53. KUBIE, LAWRENCE S., "A Fortieth Reunion in 2156," *Harvard Alumni Bulletin*, LIX (September 29, 1956), 2-4.

54. KUBIE, LAWRENCE S., "The Use of Psychoanalysis as a Research Tool," in *Psychiatric Research Reports*, No. 6, American Psychiatric Association (October, 1956), pp. 112-136.

55. KUBIE, LAWRENCE S., "On Preconscious Processes," etc., read before American Academy of Neurology, April, 1957. In press.

56. LINDLEY, DONALD, "Basic Perceptual Processes and the Electroencephalogram," in *Psychiatric Research Reports*, No. 6, American Psychiatric Association (January, 1956), 161-171.

57. LOMBROSO, C., *Genie und Irrsin*, tr. Courth, A., Berlin, 1910.

58. LOMBROSO, C., *Genio e Degenerazione*, Palermo, Sicily, 1897.

59. LOMBROSO, C., *Man of Genius*, London, 1901.

60. LOMBROSO, C., *Studies on Genius and Degeneration*, tr. Jentsch, Ernst, Reclam. 1910.

147

61. MARSH, JAMES T., and WORDEN, F. G., "Perceptual Approaches to Personality," in *Psychiatric Research Reports*, No. 6, American Psychiatric Association (January, 1956), 171-177.

62. MURPHY, LOIS, unpublished data, personal communication.

62A. LOEWENFELD, VICTOR, *Creative and Mental Growth*, third edition, New York, 1957.

63. NAUMBURG, MARGARET, "Studies of the Free Art Expression of Behavior Problem Children and Adolescents as a Means of Diagnosis and Therapy," *Nervous and Mental Disease Monographs*, No. 71, New York, 1947.

64. NAUMBURG, MARGARET, *Schizophrenic Art, Its Meaning in Psychotherapy*, New York, 1950.

65. NAUMBURG, MARGARET, *Psychoneurotic Art, Its Function in Psychotherapy*, New York, 1953.

66. NICOLE, CHARLES, *Biologie de L'Invention*, Librairie Felix Alcan, Paris, 1932.

67. OBERNDORF, CLARENCE P., *The Psychiatric Novels of Oliver Wendell Holmes*, New York, 1943.

68. PHILLIPS, WILLIAM (ed.), *Art and Psychoanalysis*, New York, 1957.

69. "Revue de Synthése. Transactions of the 9th Semaine de Synthése," *L'Invention*, XIV (October, 1937), 167-171.

70. RICHET, CHARLES, *The Natural History of a Savant*, tr. Sir Oliver Lodge, London, 1927. (Original French edition, 1923.)

71. SACHS, HANNS, *The Creative Unconscious* (second and last edition), Cambridge, Mass., 1942-1951.

72. SPITZ, RENÉ, *Hospitalism. The Psychoanalytic Study of the Child*, New York, 1945-1947, 53-75; II, 113-119; III, 53-75.

73. STERBA, RICHARD and EDITHA, *Beethoven and his Nephew*, New York, 1954.

74. TAUSK, V., "On the Origin of the 'Influencing Machine' in Schizophrenia," *Psychoanalytic Quarterly*, II (1933), 519-556.

75. TOLMAN, RICHARD, "Physical Science and Philosophy," *The Scientific Monthly*, LVII (August, 1943), 166-174.

76. TRILLING, LIONEL, *Freud and the Crisis of Our Culture*, Boston, 1955.

77. WHYTE, LANCELOT LAW, *Aspects of Form: A Symposium on Form in Nature and Art*, New York, 1951.

Index

Conscious symbol: communication necessarily slower than by coded signals of preconscious processes, 25; as instrument for sampling preconscious stream, 25; pedestrian in contrast to the coded signal of preconscious process, 24; as economizing instrument, 24; literal samples for purposes of communication, rumination, and self-critique, 23

Creative people: hypothetical vulnerability, 4; dissimilarity in lives of creative artists and scientists not paralleled by dissimilarity in the creative process itself, 96-98; changing demands in different phases of scientific creativity, 80-82

Creative process: vulnerability in relation to symbolic process, 5; distorted by universal neurotic ingredient in human nature, 7-10 passim; distortion and imprisonment by unconscious forces, 62-64

Creativity: unrecognized in the common man, 2; failure to protect against or resolve the neurotic process, 2; and the dream, 3; not dependent upon psychopathology, 4; quantitative reduction under impact of neurotic process, 6; stereotype under impact of neurotic process, 6; qualitative distortions imposed by neurotic process, 6; attempt to clarify the role of neurosis in life, 10-11; its essential nature, 50-51; and free association, 53, 54; cultural impotence due to neurotic distortion, 6; cultural consequences of its distortion and imprisonment by unconscious processes, 64-65; conflicting ambivalent impulses, expressed through identical acts in science and in art, 98-103

—and neurotic process: universality of both, 1; origins, 1; relation to symbolic process, 5; relationship to educational process, 1, 17-19, 104-122, 127; simultaneous attempt to express and to mask unconscious forces, 11; joint dependence on dissociation of thinking, feeling, and action, 17; dissociation of organized behavior into fragmented elements of thought, feeling, and action essential to both creativity and neurosis, 17-19 passim

—distortions under the influence of the impact of the unconscious on preconscious processes: examples from finance, 74-77, 103; examples from scientific research, 78-83; examples from science, 83-86; examples from literature and the plastic arts, 89-90; parallels between representative art and literature and applied science on the one hand, and non-representational art or literature and pure science on the other, 93-96

Dream: as an art form, 3; as precipitant of illness, 3; as illustration of the interplay of conscious and preconscious processes, with and without distortions from impact of unconscious processes, 66-74 passim

Education and Neurosis:

—Learning process: dependence upon repetition, automatic preconscious imitation, identification, and differentiation between internal and external worlds, 17-19 passim; challenge to find ways to free the latent preconscious capacities inherent in all men from interference and distortion by unconscious forces, 104-110

—Communication and education: need for methods to eliminate interference and distortion from unconscious processes, 104-110; interference with free preconscious functions, 110-111; lack of correlation between education and maturity, 111-112

—Indices of cultural failure: human nature unchanged, failure to transmit the fruits of experience from generation to generation, failure to free latent preconscious potential, 113-115; limited correlation between education and maturity, 111-112; the persistent immaturity of the scholar, 128-132

Appendix

Notes added for this edition.

* PAGE 11

There are several ingredients of the learning process without which learning is impossible. Comparing is one of these. Where men in general shrink from making comparisons about any aspects of human nature, this area remains impervious to progress or change. Consequently, the deep-seated tendency of men to hide from themselves and from one another their struggles with the neurotic ingredients in their make-up (as though it were an occasion for shame) has restricted to a small group such knowledge of the neurotic process as we are slowly winning. Yet a general appreciation of the universal masked neurotic ingredients in "normal" human nature (and particularly in the gifted) would make possible a profound cultural advance. This is where the creative craftsman in art and literature would come into his own, and would help to deepen man's understanding of himself. What for most men is buried and inaccessible (i.e. "unconscious" in the technical psychoanalytical sense) is more readily accessible to many artists. Therefore they should be able to clarify for the average man both the underlying conflicts out of which neurotic troubles arise and the influence of these neurotic processes on human life.

Actually, whether he realizes it or not, when any artist or writer attempts to express the neurotic components in his own nature, he is reaching for this high goal; and his attempt commands respect and gratitude even when he is not wholly successful. Nor should we be surprised or angered when he fails; since this very failure is a measure of the immaturity of our culture as a whole and of the inadequacy of the educational processes to which all of us, artists included, are exposed. Sometimes this is manifested in the confusions of the creative writer or artist about those neurotic ingredients in his own life which he is trying to express. Or his failure may be due to the strength of our reluctance to understand anything as painful as that with which he is trying to challenge us. The analyst knows how hard it is to communicate insights such as this to one person at a time, to wit, one patient. It is hardly surprising that the task of the creative artist is even harder, when he challenges men en masse to look at these same aspects of themselves without averting their eyes. Blocked and confused by these obstacles, both internal and external, the artist often makes unwitting compromises, which end by obscuring instead of clarifying the essential nature of the struggles which he is attempting to represent. This, in turn, is one reason why the creative product, like the neurotic symptom, usually masks more than it illuminates, even when it is skillful and moving.

These compromises are of many kinds. Thus the goriest or lustiest sexual melodrama or comedy contains elements of truth; but in a form which goes so far beyond the range of ordinary human experience that the audience reacts to it with feelings of mingled fascination, horror and pleasure. Yet at the same time each member of that audience is enabled by the artist's exaggerations to feel that it is something so alien to him that, "It cannot happen here. It has nothing to do with me." This is a familiar defense, to sit and stew in complicated emotional juices with a mixture of pleasure, pain and distance. Portraying universal human struggles in a form which makes each living man feel that this is an alien experience cannot add to his insights either into himself or into human nature in general. Alternatively, to dilute the full impact of some painful human struggle by the use of humor or any other form of sugarcoating is another way of pretending to look at something, while actually looking the other way.

I do not pretend to know the answer to this problem. I do not possess any pat formula for communicating to the many those painful inner problems from the contemplation of which every individual flees. Nevertheless, to face up to this problem focuses our attention on it as one of the unsolved basic problems of the arts and literature. Its ultimate solution will make available to us, perhaps for the first time, the great contribution that art and literature can make to human culture. I repeat that this is why I sympathize deeply with the struggles of modern art and literature, even as I deplore their failures. There are formidable obstacles to success, doubly rooted in the artist's own confusions and in the age-old resistances of man to face painful truth.

* PAGE 34

"Exteroceptive" refers to sensory input from a distance from the body. "Proprioceptive" refers primarily to afferent input from the skin, muscles, joints, etc. "Enteroceptive" refers to sensory input arising primarily from within the interior of the body cavities and the internal organs.

* PAGE 36

The tachistoscope is an instrument for flashing an image on a screen for variable lengths of time, sometimes too brief for conscious recognition of anything except that there was a flash of light with some marks on it.